GOING ALT-AC

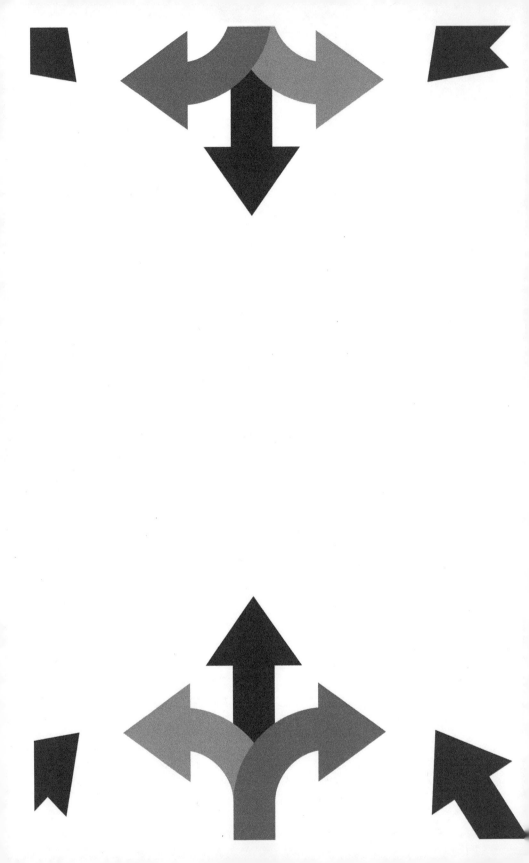

GOING ALT-AC

A Guide to Alternative Academic Careers

Kathryn E. Linder, Kevin Kelly, and Thomas J. Tobin

Foreword by Joshua Kim

STERLING, VIRGINIA

Published by Stylus Publishing, LLC.
22883 Quicksilver Drive
Sterling, Virginia 20166-2019

Library of Congress Cataloging-in-Publication Data
Names: Linder, Kathryn E., author. | Kelly, Kevin (Kevin Matthew), author. |
    Tobin, Thomas J., author. | Kim, Joshua, 1969- writer of foreword.
Title: Going alt-ac : a guide to alternative academic careers / Kathryn E. Linder,
    Kevin Kelly and Thomas J. Tobin ; foreword by Joshua Kim.
Other titles: Going alternative-academic
Description: Sterling, Virginia : Stylus, 2020. | Includes bibliographical references
    and index.
Identifiers: LCCN 2019048889 (print) | LCCN 2019048890 (ebook) | ISBN
    9781620368305 (hardcover) | ISBN 9781620368312 (paperback) | ISBN
    9781620368329 (pdf) | ISBN 9781620368336 (ebook)
Subjects: LCSH: Job hunting. | Graduate students--Employment. | Career changes.
Classification: LCC HF5382.7 .L556 2020 (print) | LCC HF5382.7 (ebook) |
    DC 650.14--dc23
LC record available at https://lccn.loc.gov/2019048889
LC ebook record available at https://lccn.loc.gov/2019048890

13-digit ISBN: 978-1-62036-830-5 (cloth)
13-digit ISBN: 978-1-62036-831-2 (paperback)
13-digit ISBN: 978-1-62036-832-9 (library networkable e-edition)
13-digit ISBN: 978-1-62036-833-6 (consumer e-edition)

Printed in the United States of America

All first editions printed on acid-free paper
that meets the American National Standards Institute
Z39-48 Standard.

Bulk Purchases

Quantity discounts are available for use in workshops and for staff development.

Call 1-800-232-0223

First Edition, 2020

CONTENTS

FOREWORD

oing Alt-Ac is a book that will change lives. If that sounds like too strong an endorsement, then you are not one of us trying to navigate an alternative academic (alt-ac) career. If *Going Alt-Ac* had been available 20 years ago, as I began my own post-PhD nontraditional academic journey, then I think the book would have saved me from years of career angst. Among the many beautiful things that *Going Alt-Ac* accomplishes is to give those of us pursuing nonlinear post-PhD paths the understanding that we are not alone. That our choices to pursue something outside of a faculty role are legitimate. And that it is okay, even maybe universal, for those in alt-ac to feel as if we are making up our careers as we go.

The main message of *Going Alt-Ac* is that one need not follow a traditional faculty path to have a rewarding and impactful academic career. As this book explains, for many PhDs, an alt-ac career will be the best choice. How might a life of alternative academia possibly be preferable to the tenure track? The world of nontraditional academic careers combines many of the best things about being a professor with the benefits of life outside of academia. An alt-ac gig means trading the life of a super subspecialist for that of a generalist. Alt-acs work with partners from every discipline. Where in many academic disciplines the scholarship on which career advancement depends can be solitary (particularly in the humanities), alt-ac careers are collaborative by nature. Alt-acs work mostly in teams.

Although those on the nontraditional, nontenure, academic track will often continue to produce scholarship, they tend to do so in different ways. Without the demand to publish in only peer-reviewed journals or university presses, alt-acs are perhaps more free than traditional faculty to integrate their scholarship with public outreach and engagement. *Going Alt-Ac* takes the reader step-by-step through how early career alt-acs can build up their professional reputations and communities of practice through engaging in professional associations, social media, and consulting. These are all activities that are valued by the broader alt-ac community and that offer creative platforms for professional growth.

Another gift of *Going Alt-Ac*, both for those of us in our second decade of a nontraditional academic career and for those who may be just starting down this path, is the book's avoidance of happy talk. As the authors recognize and discuss, alt-ac careers can be immensely rewarding, but they are seldom easy. Those of us on the outside of the well-worn faculty path often find ourselves on the margins of our institutions. *Going Alt-Ac* does a terrific job of capturing the liminal nature of nontraditional academic careers. Existing somewhere between staff and faculty, alt-acs operate in the gray areas of the academy. The simple act of filling out the "occupation" section of a form is a challenge for alt-acs: There is no job category that starts with "alternative."

The authors produced a book that anyone contemplating, or negotiating, a nontraditional academic career will want to read. Readers will want to not only read but also workshop and teach and share. When I was growing up, my parents were part of a loose counterculture of vegetarian academics. I remember a defining feature of this subgroup was how all of these alternative food people seemed to own a dog-eared copy of *The Moosewood Cookbook*. First self-published in 1974 by Mollie Katzen, *The Moosewood Cookbook* went on to inspire a generation of new vegetarians, while giving those who had already stopped eating meat one of the first reliable and accessible guides to cooking delicious food. I suspect that *Going Alt-Ac* will be the *Moosewood* for this generation's growing number of nontraditional academics. I think that we will keep *Going Alt-Ac* on our desks, as both a reference guide and a reminder that we are part of something bigger. We will give the book to our advisers and faculty colleagues. When our partners and our parents and our friends ask what we do for a living, we will answer confidently that we are "going alt-ac."

Joshua Kim, PhD
Director of Digital Learning Initiatives,
Dartmouth College Center for the Advancement of Learning

PREFACE

Is This the Book for You? (Spoiler Alert: It Is)

Are you completing, or do you already hold, a graduate degree? If so, then you are among a growing number of people who may pursue an alternative academic, or *alt-ac*, position at some stage in their career. An increasing number of us have completed the preparation to become faculty members in colleges and universities, but there aren't enough of those faculty jobs to go around. Or maybe you have decided that the traditional faculty pathway isn't for you. This book is a combination of how-to advice, inspiring stories, and thought exercises that will help you explore the alt-ac job market, navigate common challenges, and find rewarding work that honors your skills and knowledge, regardless of whether you are completing your postgraduate studies now or you have already been in the workforce for a while after earning your degree.

Going Alt-Ac is not meant to be a scholarly treatise. All three of the authors are scholars and researchers, and you will find plenty of support and data for the ideas and practices for which we advocate throughout this book. However, our goal is not to create a dry piece of analysis; rather, this book is a practical, hands-on guide to the wide and engaging field of alt-ac work. We wrote this book because we have been there: we were trained by our PhD programs to become faculty members in our disciplines, but we each ended up seeking different pathways within higher education.

Many of us who became alt-ac practitioners at the beginning of the twenty-first century did so with little guidance and a lot of experimentation. We wrote this book because it is what we wish we had when we were first starting out. This book is meant to help you create a meaningful path toward work that you are proud of, that aligns with your values, and that uses your knowledge and skills. Over time, we discovered that we were not alone in our alt-ac career seeking. Along the way in this book, you will meet many people who have walked down this path successfully.

Who Are Alt-Acs?

Broadening slightly the definition from Bethany Nowviskie, Katina Rogers, and their colleagues, we could define *academics alternative* as "people with graduate training in [any discipline] who apply their skills to a wide spectrum of positions beyond the tenure-track" (Rogers, n.d.). In fact, a lack of available tenure-track positions in many disciplines is one of the primary reasons for the increased interest in alt-ac careers.

The term *alt-ac* is a little slippery. The idea of alt-ac work contains a wide variety of roles, perhaps because the very term itself is defined in opposition to something: *Alt-ac* is what you do when you cannot obtain—or do not want—a tenure-line faculty position, but you have been trained, by and large, to be a faculty member. So far, these definitions are less than helpful and could even be mildly rude to some of our colleagues, such as our librarian friends who do not perceive their work as a fallback field for disappointed PhDs (we have seen many articles that take just such a tone).

We alt-acs are a diverse group: teaching center staff, scientists and researchers, professional consultants, museum workers, nonprofit staff members, corporate trainers, administrators, and more. Bethman and Longstreet (2013) offered a useful working definition of *alt-ac positions*: "full-time non-teaching and non-research positions within higher education" (para. 3). Indeed, a mark of a flourishing new field is its ability to codify, nourish, and pass along norms and best practices for new members of the field (Brown, 2016, p. 34). Many PhD programs and scholarly organizations are coming to terms with the idea that they must provide broader guidance to their students and membership, respectively, in regard to job prospects beyond professorships (Flint & Phillips, 2018; Kuhn & Castaño, 2016). What ties us together is our initial training, and that common bond can help us see ourselves as a professional field.

Throughout this book, we purposely simplify the very broad space of possible postgraduate-training work into the following three categories, each defined by how many steps they are removed from the ivory-tower faculty positions that many PhD programs have trained us to fill:

1. Academic positions: These are faculty, researcher, and instructor positions within colleges and universities.
2. Alt-ac positions: These are jobs in which people with advanced degrees serve colleges and universities but not in traditional faculty roles or jobs in which people's work in nonacademic institutions serves academic and scholarly goals.
3. Non-ac positions: These are positions outside colleges and universities in which advanced-degree holders are applying the skills they obtained during their studies in a range of creative ways. In some fields, we often just call this "working in industry."

We recognize that our ac–alt-ac–non-ac framework risks presenting a flowing continuum of job choices as distinct categories; these are not totally separate and don't require totally different training, and many people pursue job searches in many career areas across the spectrum we present here. That said, we will explain why these distinctions are helpful for job preparation, early- and mid-career strategic shifts, and advocacy for broader conversations from those of us well established in our alt-ac careers.

How to Read This Book

Going Alt-Ac has the following parts, roughly corresponding to stages of the alt-ac career cycle:

- Part One: An Introduction to Going Alt-Ac
- Part Two: Exploring Alt-Ac Careers
- Part Three: Getting Started in Alt-Ac
- Part Four: Addressing Common Alt-Ac Challenges
- Part Five: Growing in the Alt-Ac Space
- Part Six: Building Your Alt-Ac Presence
- Part Seven: The Alt-Ac Career Life Cycle

Because many ideas and decisions in our careers look different from varying vantage points, you'll notice that a number of the chapters within each section echo each other or cover similar concepts; that's on purpose, to help readers at many stages of their alt-ac experiences.

While we hope that you will enjoy reading this book from the numerical and data-supported overview of chapter 1 right through to the conclusion, we also suggest reading certain chapters first, based on the stage of your career, your eventual career goals, and what types of jobs you're looking to obtain. And if you're unsure about any of those categories, we have you covered, too. Look to Table P.1 for a suggested reading-order chart for various readers of *Going Alt-Ac*.

How to Use This Book

We organized this book according to key decision points along alt-ac career time lines, including those that involve people who began in traditional faculty or nonfaculty careers. We also made sure to address the needs of every

TABLE P.1
Suggested Reading Order

	Current Graduate Students	Looking for a Mid-Career Job Switch	Part-Time Alt-Ac Work Wanted	Graduate Adviser/ Peer Mentor
Part One: An Introduction to Going Alt-Ac				
1: Why Go Alt-Ac?	✓	✓	✓	
2: Who Considers Alt-Ac Careers?	✓	✓		✓
Part Two: Exploring Alt-Ac Careers				
3: Do You Want to Work in Higher Ed?	✓	✓		
4: Alt-Ac Opportunities Outside Academia	✓	✓		✓
5: Being Aware of Emotions When Making Career Decisions	✓			
6: Mapping an Alt-Ac Career Trajectory	✓			
7: Learning More About Alt-Ac Fields	✓		✓	✓
Part Three: Getting Started in Alt-Ac				
8: Preparing for an Alt-Ac Career While Still in Grad School	✓			
9: Getting Your Partner or Family on Board With the Decision to Go Alt-Ac	✓	✓		
10: Communicating About Alt-Ac Careers With Graduate Advisers	✓			✓
11: Job Hunting	✓	✓		
12: Preparing Alt-Ac Job Materials	✓	✓		✓
13: Interviewing	✓	✓		
Part Four: Addressing Common Alt-Ac Challenges				
14: Addressing the Two-Body Problem	✓	✓		

(*Continues*)

TABLE P.1 (*Continued*)

	Current Graduate Students	Looking for a Mid-Career Job Switch	Part-Time Alt-Ac Work Wanted	Graduate Adviser/ Peer Mentor
15: Finding a Niche and an Appropriate Audience	✓		✓	✓
16: Communicating How Disciplinary Knowledge and Skills Support Work in Specific Alt-Ac Roles	✓		✓	✓
17: Making Good Use of a Dissertation After Graduation	✓			✓
18: Establishing Credibility When Getting Started	✓			✓
19: Having Effective Conversations	✓	✓	✓	
Part Five: Growing in the Alt-Ac Space				
20: Doing Consulting Work			✓	✓
21: Working Up Internally or Moving Up by Moving On		✓		
22: Writing and Publishing		✓	✓	✓
23: Joining and Participating in Professional Organizations	✓	✓	✓	✓
Part Six: Building Your Alt-Ac Presence				
24: Getting Experience	✓			✓
25: Building a Portfolio Over Time and With Intentionality		✓	✓	
26: Finding a Sponsor or Mentoring Group to Help	✓	✓		
27: Creating and Growing a Personal Brand		✓	✓	
Part Seven: The Alt-Ac Career Life Cycle				
28: From Alt-Ac to Faculty Roles	✓			✓

(*Continues*)

TABLE P.1   *(Continued)*

	Current Graduate Students	Looking for a Mid-Career Job Switch	Part-Time Alt-Ac Work Wanted	Graduate Adviser/ Peer Mentor
29: From Faculty to Alt-Ac Roles		✓		✓
30: Part-Time Alt-Ac Roles		✓	✓	
31: Be an Alt-Ac Mentor		✓	✓	✓
Conclusion	✓	✓	✓	✓

alt-ac job seeker, including those who have chosen the alt-ac pathway intentionally and purposefully. As a whole, this book outlines the challenges and benefits of pursuing alt-ac career paths and offers tips and suggestions for how to enter into and thrive in alt-ac roles.

Going Alt-Ac: A Guide to Alternative Academic Careers focuses on alt-ac career choices made by increasing numbers of graduate students and academics. This book is highly practical, providing tools and prompts for readers who are considering whether to choose an alt-ac career path, seeking specific alt-ac positions, advising graduate students or mentoring recent professional graduates, or encountering alt-ac career challenges.

Each part in this book begins with a list of outcomes that you will be prepared to achieve; poses guiding questions for different stakeholder groups such as graduate students, recent graduates, graduate advisers, and those in academia considering a career shift; and helps you examine your skill sets and pivot your presentation, language, and approach as you engage in your alt-ac career exploration.

This book also discusses methods for growing your alt-ac network, building your alt-ac professional identity, and more. To ground the book, we offer case stories—our own and those of veteran colleagues in various professional alt-ac roles across North America—with concrete examples designed to help you pursue, obtain, and excel in a wide variety of alt-ac positions. People who enjoy variety and complexity in their work will thrive in the alt-ac career space; we are excited to provide this book as a resource for wherever you are in your own alt-ac journey.

ACKNOWLEDGMENTS

This book would not have been possible without the generosity and support of colleagues throughout the United States and Canada. The authors wish to thank the myriad people at colleges, universities, and advocacy organizations; the vendors; and those in government who made time to talk with us, share their stories, and explain their research. Because this book provides a combination of evidence-based practices, case studies, and theoretical advice, we are indebted to the hard work of our colleagues who are proving every day that alt-ac work is vital, meaningful, and rewarding.

We could not fit all of their stories into this book. Their ideas nonetheless inform our writing and our conclusions. Of course, any infelicities in the text are our own. We are especially grateful to the following people for their willingness to share their work and ideas with us over the past several years: Chris Cloney, Andrea Colangelo, Michele DiPietro, Brad Franklin, Carl Grossman, Erin Hoag, Hoag Holmgren, Valerie Kisiel, Sara Langworthy, David Laurence, Ruth Nemire, Lindsay Padilla, Charity Peak, David Peak, Pam Ranallo, Beth Seltzer, Lee Skallerup Bessette, James Van Wyck, John Whitmer, Michael Wing, and Todd Zakrajsek.

A huge thanks to Joshua Kim for writing the book's foreword and for being such a tireless advocate for the alt-ac community. Also, many thanks to the dedicated team at Stylus Publishing. A special thank-you to our editor, David Brightman, for ushering this book through the various stages of review and revision toward publication; we have appreciated your insights, support, and thoughtful questions along the way.

PART ONE

AN INTRODUCTION TO
GOING ALT-AC

I n Part One, we outline key aspects of alt-ac careers. Chapter 1 describes why someone would want to pursue an alt-ac career, depicts the alt-ac career space, and lists some of the employment opportunities within it. In chapter 2, we review who might choose an alt-ac career.

I

WHY GO ALT-AC?

In this chapter, you will (a) review the entire spectrum of career choices doctoral graduates might make, focusing on what constitutes an alt-ac career, and (b) outline realistic employment opportunities in both academic and alt-ac positions.

Motivation for Choosing an Alt-Ac Position or Career

Whether you are working toward a doctoral or terminal degree, or have already earned one, you are used to forming conclusions based on research. Those who prefer quantitative data may want to start with some numbers, and those numbers speak to a limited number of academic career options. First, we can look at the total number of available positions in higher education environments. According to the National Center for Education Statistics (NCES), there were just under 4 million jobs at 6,636 postsecondary institutions in fall 2016; almost 1 million more than existed in fall 2002. Of those fall 2016 jobs, however, only 15% of them (0.6 million) were full-time, instructional staff positions at 4,159 institutions (NCES, 2018). It is interesting to note that full-time teaching positions are not even available at more than one-third of higher education institutions.

Second, we can look at trends related to the numbers of academic and alt-ac teaching positions. The U.S. Government Accountability Office (2017) found that the number of tenure-track positions grew only 9.6% over 16 years (from 1995 to 2011), while the numbers of full-time and part-time contingent positions each grew by over 100%. Analysis of NCES data by the American Association of University Professors (AAUP) showed that "non-tenure-track positions of all types now account for over 70 percent of all instructional staff appointments in American higher education" (AAUP, 2016, para. 3), referencing both part- and full-time appointments.

Third, we can track trends related to the number of people who might seek academic or alt-ac positions. In a comparable time span, the number of people earning doctoral degrees each year quadrupled, from 44,160 in 2001–2002 to 177,867 in 2015–2016 (NCES, 2018). To put it plainly, every year there are more people who may be competing for fewer available academic positions.

As these numbers show, many PhDs are now turning to adjunct positions to develop their teaching skills, follow their passion for teaching, or both. However, people often must combine non-tenure-track teaching with other types of academic work to make ends meet. The U.S. Government Accountability Office (2017) conducted an in-depth study in three states—Georgia, North Dakota, and Ohio—and found that full-time faculty were paid 10% less per course and part-time contingent faculty were paid 60% less per course than tenure-track faculty. A summary of data from a 2012 Coalition on the Academic Workforce study of over 10,000 part-time, contingent faculty found that

> many adjuncts have to work multiple jobs in order to make enough money to subsist—and even then, more than half of them make less than $35,000 a year (and many of those who make more do so only because they have second jobs outside of academia). (Edmonds, 2015, para. 6)

Graduates and academics choose alt-ac positions for a variety of reasons, and many of these reasons do not involve the availability of academic positions. Regardless of their motivation, many of them want to work in an academic setting. Luckily, while the numbers of tenure-track faculty positions are decreasing, the staff and administrative ranks in higher education institutions are growing. With increased concerns about compliance regarding a range of federal and state requirements related to disability, access, equity, and other concerns, as well as the changing needs of a diverse student population, colleges and universities are creating a wide range of positions that support teaching and learning, scholarly development, and other efforts.

An Overview of Alt-Ac Positions

On many campuses, alt-ac positions typically fall into one of the following categories: student affairs or student services; academic affairs; advancement, development, and research; and administration, finance, and business affairs. Jobs and careers within these categories often direct their efforts to serving the specific needs of (a) the learners, from admissions to advising to alumni relations; (b) the teachers, such as educational development, scholarship and grant development, or educational technology; (c) the institution as a whole, such as fund-raising or institutional research; or (d) the communities served by the institution, such as public affairs, civic engagement, and communications.

Beyond campuses, alt-ac positions exist at organizations focused on supporting or advancing academic goals in higher education, such as higher education district or system offices, nonprofit organizations, research institutes, government agencies, companies, and start-ups. Roles at these organizations may develop policies or products for, or provide services to, higher education institutions; they may also work with those institutions to move broader academic initiatives forward. As individuals, alt-ac professionals and some academics may also engage in part-time or full-time alt-ac roles through publishing, public speaking, consulting, or some combination of these activities. Figure 1.1 depicts many, but not all, of the alt-ac positions that you might consider and shows those positions in the context of both the academic-to-nonacademic spectrum and a potential career span.

As you review this panoply of career choices, you may identify a need for additional preparation. PhDs who have been trained in specific disciplines may need new skills, or may need to rethink the skills they already have, to compete for these new positions. Problematically, while an increasing number of people with doctoral degrees are hunting for a diminishing pool of tenure-track faculty jobs, most degree-granting institutions do not adequately prepare their graduate students to enter the new reality of the alt-ac job market. Moreover, some mid-career PhDs are unfamiliar with the newer landscape of alt-ac roles. Continue to chapter 2 to find out more about these aspects of the alt-ac field.

Figure 1.1. The alt-ac career space.

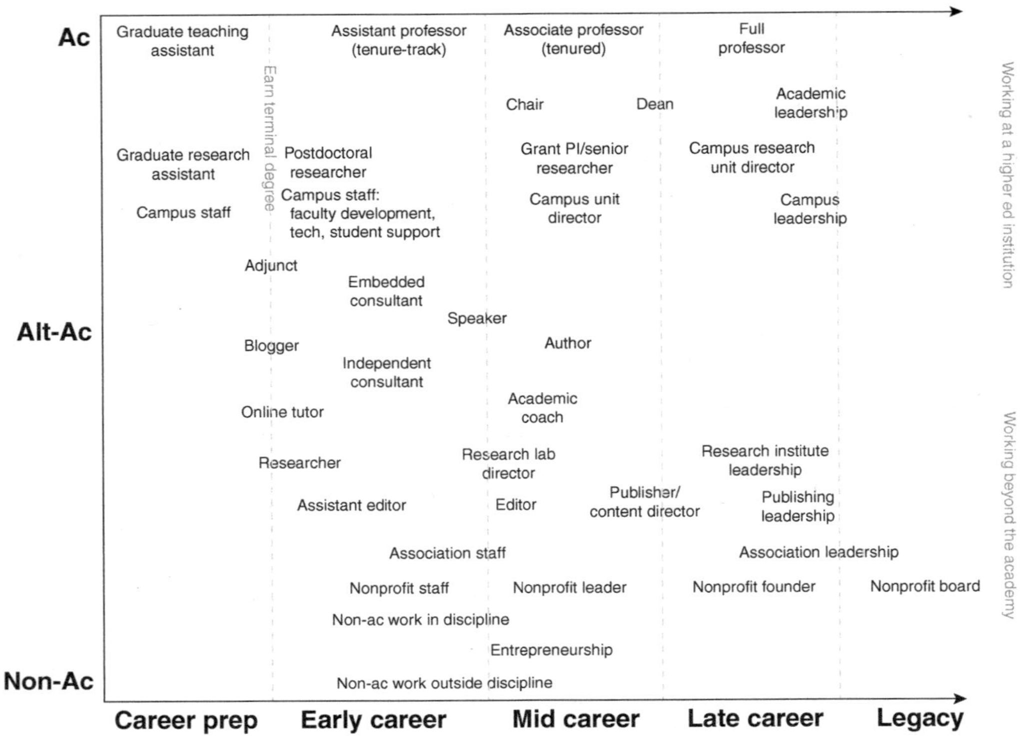

Working at a higher ed institution   Working beyond the academy

Ac

Graduate teaching assistant

Graduate research assistant

Campus staff

Adjunct

Postdoctoral researcher

Campus staff: faculty development, tech, student support

Embedded consultant

Speaker

Assistant professor (tenure-track)

Chair

Dean

Associate professor (tenured)

Grant PI/senior researcher

Campus unit director

Campus research unit director

Full professor

Academic leadership

Campus leadership

Earn terminal degree

Alt-Ac

Blogger

Independent consultant

Online tutor

Researcher

Assistant editor

Academic coach

Author

Research lab director

Editor

Publisher/ content director

Research institute leadership

Publishing leadership

Non-Ac

Association staff

Nonprofit staff

Non-ac work in discipline

Entrepreneurship

Non-ac work outside discipline

Nonprofit leader

Association leadership

Nonprofit founder

Nonprofit board

Career prep   Early career   Mid career   Late career   Legacy

2

WHO CONSIDERS ALT-AC CAREERS?

In this chapter, you will identify the populations for whom alt-ac pathways present viable and meaningful career opportunities.

Different Starting Points Along the Alt-Ac Path

As we mentioned in the previous chapter, people consider alt-ac careers at various points along their career paths. People in the middle or at the end of the career preparation stage include current graduate students and recent graduates. These people want to enter an academic environment after earning a doctoral or terminal degree, but they either do not want or must wait to pursue tenure-track faculty positions. Does this sound like you? There are a variety of reasons why you might pursue an alt-ac path rather than take the tenure track.

For example, are you more interested in a specific alt-ac role that would take advantage of your unique skill set, now or after you graduate? Are there no tenure-track opportunities in your geographic area, and/or are you not in a position to relocate right now? Do you need to postpone a tenure-track job search until your partner finishes a degree? Whatever your reason may be, many people who earn a doctoral or terminal degree want to work in the academic arena beyond the tenure track, and there are plenty of alt-ac positions that will allow you to do just that.

Another group—those in their early career stage—discovers alt-ac roles as an option while working in short-term positions after earning a degree. Have you decided that a faculty role is not for you while serving as a post-doctoral fellow? Have you been seeking faculty positions after your graduate studies while working in several temporary, part-time jobs—sequentially or simultaneously—and now want to explore a permanent, full-time position?

Alt-ac positions and careers provide potential avenues to support early career transitions.

Yet another group includes mid-career-stage professionals who are in nonacademic roles but want to move to an academic environment. Are you in a place in your career where you want to share what you have learned with future leaders and workers in your field? Do you feel a calling to serve a more educationally focused mission? Do you miss the academic or campus vibe you felt when you worked on your graduate degree(s)? If any of these reasons ring true, then an alt-ac position may be for you.

A final, much smaller group considering alt-ac careers is made up of people in the mid-career, late career, and even legacy stages—tenure-track or tenured faculty who no longer want to serve in that capacity or faculty who are about to retire but want to stay in an academic environment. If this describes you, you are not alone. Has your work on a committee or with a community-based organization inspired you to take on a new role? Has the institution tapped you to take a leadership role in the administration? Have funding sources for your research dried up because of changes in governmental policy or a shift in a foundation's mission? If your decision is driven by a desire to start something new, devote more time and energy to a side gig, or stop performing certain aspects of your tenure-track role, then the alt-ac path offers you a chance to stay connected to the academic world.

Next Steps

Are you still not sure if alt-ac positions are right for you? You are in luck. If you are a graduate student or recent graduate, start with your campus career center. Talk to a career counselor and ask any questions you have as you read this book. In later chapters we will cover interviewing alt-ac professionals at your institution. Beyond on-campus resources, there are free and for-fee discipline-based online career decision tools for PhDs. These tools include useful resources such as assessments to determine career-related interests, background knowledge, skills, and attitudes; annotated lists of potential jobs in different areas; samples of items you may need to create (e.g., cover letters); and planning instruments to guide goal setting and progress tracking. These tools include, but are not limited to, the following:

- MyIDP is a free online career-decision tool for people with degrees in science, technology, engineering, and math (STEM) fields (myidp .sciencecareers.org). *Science* magazine also produced a series of articles about MyIDP (www.sciencemag.org/careers/2012/09/ you-need-game-plan).

- ImaginePhD is a free online career-decision tool for people with degrees in the humanities and social sciences (www.imaginephd .com).
- Options4Success offers a for-fee career explorations course (www .beyondthetenuretrack.com/options). Unlike MyIDP and Imagine PhD, this option provides opportunities to interact with people who can help you with your decision-making process.
- The Versatile PhD is a large online community dedicated to "helping graduate students and PhDs envision, prepare for, and excel in non-academic careers" (versatilephd.com).
- From PhD to Life includes a Beyond the Professoriate community, a Self-Employed PhD network, and one-on-one support services to help people set and achieve career goals (fromphdtolife.com).

PART TWO

EXPLORING ALT-AC CAREERS

In Part Two, we review alt-ac positions found at most higher education institutions in areas related to academic support, student support, research, administration, community relations, and more. We also share a variety of alt-ac career opportunities beyond higher education campuses in diverse locations such as publishing houses, technology firms, nonprofit organizations, and research institutes.

Recognizing that some doctoral graduates want tenure-track faculty positions, we offer these individuals strategies for coping with the need to change career directions and for turning that need to their advantage. After outlining these aspects of alt-ac careers, we offer suggestions for mapping your own alt-ac career trajectory. Finally, we provide ideas for learning more about alt-ac careers or positions that interest you.

3

DO YOU WANT TO WORK IN HIGHER ED?

In this chapter, you will (a) consider in more detail alt-ac careers or positions at or serving higher education institutions and (b) explore questions designed to determine if working at a higher education institution is the correct alt-ac career path for you.

Choosing to Work on a College or University Campus

If you've made the decision to work in higher education, an important consideration is whether or not to work on a campus. Let's start with some of the pros. While higher education institutions do face budget and staff cutbacks, working at those institutions has generally been more stable compared to the overall U.S. job market (HigherEdJobs, 2013). Once you get an on-campus position, there can be opportunities for lateral moves and upward advancement. Moreover, campus units often must weigh hiring decisions in favor of people who already work at that institution.

Working directly on a campus can provide a variety of benefits. Depending on the institution, these benefits can include convenient access to and discounted rates for athletic or wellness facilities; consistent, annual time off during holiday campus closures; access to library resources and services; on-campus child care programs; tuition fee waiver programs for employees, spouses, and/or children; housing assistance; and retirement funding (T. Williams, n.d.).

To be transparent, there are cons that counteract some of the pros. For example, while jobs at colleges and universities are considered more stable, some positions rank lower in average pay in relation to comparable positions at for-profit companies. While campuses offer many benefits, they can sometimes lag behind the corporate world in areas like workplace technology. Compared to decisions in the business world, decisions on campus tend to take longer to make and implement. However, many higher education employees feel that better work–life balance, increased job security, and stronger retirement benefits outweigh higher education's lower pay rates, older technology systems, or slower processes.

Categories and Types of Alt-Ac Positions Offered by Higher Education Institutions

You might be asking yourself, "Other than faculty positions, what types of jobs can I find at colleges and universities?" and "How many of each type of job are there?" To find out, David Laurence (2016) from the Modern Language Association (MLA) Office of Research analyzed data from the Integrated Postsecondary Education Data System (IPEDS) to study higher education employment trends over a 24-year period (from 1987 to 2011). He found that (a) the support and service professionals category grew to comprise roughly 30% of full-time positions at 4-year institutions, (b) the faculty category remained flat at roughly 30%, and (c) the clerical and secretarial category dropped to less than 15% (Laurence, 2016).

Despite common complaints about administrative bloat, the executive, administrative, and managerial category grew only slightly, staying at just less than 10%. Preliminary but more recent data from fall 2017 showed that these percentages of full-time positions have not changed dramatically (Ginder, Kelly-Reid, & Mann, 2018, pp. 15–16).

Diving a little deeper, we see there is a wide variety of roles in different areas at higher education institutions. Those non-tenure-track job categories include, but are not limited to, teaching or teaching support, student support, administration, research and research support, library and information sciences, technology services, publishing, community engagement, and even entrepreneurial enterprises.

Teaching or Teaching Support Positions

Teaching or teaching support positions can include non-tenure-track faculty, K–12 principals and teachers for elementary and secondary schools run or hosted by a higher education institution, teaching center directors and staff, instructional designers, and academic technology specialists. Entry-level work may involve developing and teaching higher education courses; conducting needs assessment activities; facilitating training sessions and workshops for faculty, staff, and/or students; and creating faculty development resources. Positions require skills such as data collection and analysis; pedagogical, curriculum, and/or instructional design; in-person or virtual training facilitation; and clear communication.

Student Support Positions

Student support positions include directors or staff for student services, disability programs and resource staff, campus life and student organization professionals, health services staff, psychological counselors, academic counselors or advisers, tutoring and writing center staff, career center staff, financial aid staff, and scholarship coordinators. Entry-level work entails working directly with students in support of their academic success and social integration at the institution and their individual health and wellness.

This includes helping students with diverse backgrounds and needs as they complete academic tasks, plan and navigate their academic and professional careers, become more productive and independent individuals, engage with the campus community, and plan for the future. Positions require communication and interpersonal skills with an emphasis on patience and respect; the ability to work with adults with diverse backgrounds and needs; and the ability to develop and facilitate student support workshops, events, and programs.

Administration Positions

Campus or campus unit administration positions include college deans, administrators, and staff; academic program officers or chairs; directors or staff for academic centers and institutes; human resources; business and finance; campus safety; and development and advancement units. Entry-level work may entail coordinating personnel recruitment, interviewing, and hiring; supporting and/or managing unit or center projects; and supporting day-to-day operations. Positions require strong skills in communication, analysis, relationship-building, and organization—as well as familiarity with technologies such as employee database, payroll, and absence management systems.

Research and Research Support Positions

Research and research support positions include directors or staff of institutional research units, undergraduate research units, and research and sponsored programs units. Entry-level work may involve tasks such as analyzing complex data sets (e.g., student enrollment, financial aid, retention, course or degree completion), synthesizing information to produce reports and visualizations, responding to institutional research inquiries, supporting applications for research grants, supporting research grant awardees in evaluating progress and managing budgets, and communicating to the campus community about research topics. Positions require experience with all aspects of the research process from creating a proposal to reporting final results; strong analytical, organizational, and communication skills; and the ability to use research-related technologies.

Library and Information Sciences Positions

Library and information sciences positions include library faculty, librarians, historians, archivists, and collections or digital repository managers. Although higher level positions usually require specific degrees and experience, entry-level work entails tasks such as supporting students, faculty, and staff as they use library resources; providing training related to research and information literacy; supporting faculty and graduate students who conduct research; and managing physical or digital collections. Positions require strong oral and written communication, analytical, and problem-solving skills; experience in using research resources and learning technologies (e.g., databases); knowledge of open educational resources (OER) and other textbook affordability strategies; and the ability to lead training workshops and informational events.

Technology Services Positions

Technology services positions include systems administrators, software or web developers, media production managers and creative services staff, classroom equipment technicians and support staff, and online technology help desk staff. Entry-level work involves supporting physical and/or virtual technology environments, as well as the people who use them; collecting and analyzing data about technology use and effectiveness; and producing documentation to support campus users. Positions require the ability to communicate technical concepts to novices, maintain proficiency in using specific technologies, and solve problems.

Publishing Positions

Publishing positions, for campuses with a press or regular publications, include editors and support staff. Entry-level work entails reviewing article or book submissions, copyediting, checking references, obtaining copyright permissions, producing publications, and marketing the unit's efforts. Positions require strong skills in communicating, writing, and editing and may require knowledge of specific standards (e.g., American Psychological Association citation format) and/or technologies (e.g., desktop publishing and typesetting software).

Community Engagement Positions

Community engagement positions include directors and staff for government relations, public relations, and community engagement offices. Entry-level work involves building and maintaining relationships among public officials, chambers of commerce, community leaders, service organizations, faculty and students engaged in service-learning, and other engagement stakeholders; researching and analyzing relevant local, regional, statewide, and national policies and issues; and recommending appropriate campus actions. Positions require strong interpersonal, research, analytical, and communication skills, as well as familiarity with campus relationships with the local community.

Entrepreneurial Positions

Entrepreneurial positions include founders, leaders, and staff of start-up entities formed by a college or university. Entry-level work in this environment calls for conducting environmental scans and market analyses, creating and testing solutions, and communicating to different stakeholders in various formats. Positions require creative problem-solving, effective communication, and the abilities to work independently and to respond to changes quickly.

Categories and Types of Alt-Ac Positions That Serve Higher Education Institutions

There are also ways for people to serve one or many higher education institutions without being a direct employee. In many cases people in these roles still perform their work on a campus (or multiple campuses), even though they work for another organization or for themselves. In other cases, institutions hire consulting firms or independent consultants to get work done on campus; for example, to work around budget constraints, introduce new or outside perspectives, or fill gaps during administration or staff searches. This work can be project based and part-time or full-time, depending on the position. Positions that serve higher education institutions include job categories such as professional development, organizational development, technology services, enrollment services, business development and advancement, marketing and communications, campus administration, accreditation support, and project management.

Professional Development Positions

Professional development positions include academic technology or distance education specialists, educational developers, professional development advisers, diversity and inclusion trainers, subject matter experts, instructional designers, and pedagogical consultants. Entry-level work entails conducting needs assessment activities; facilitating training sessions and workshops for faculty, staff, and/or students; and creating instructional or professional development resources. Positions require skills such as data collection, instructional design, in-person or virtual training facilitation, and clear communication.

Organizational Development Positions

Organizational development positions include meeting or process facilitators, efficiency and process experts, and strategic planning or organizational structure consultants. Entry-level work involves tasks such as helping groups work together efficiently, analyzing and optimizing current practices, documenting plans for future work that achieves an institution's goals, and identifying and documenting the impact of organizational change on stakeholders. Positions require the ability to analyze individual and team behaviors and performance, communicate with groups and lead group activities, and translate findings into written plans or reports.

Technology Services Positions

Technology services positions include online program management professionals, technology adoption and implementation consultants, classroom technology installation and repair professionals, media production staff, network security, and help desk managers and staff. Entry-level work can range from interacting with individuals to solve technology problems and use technology to supporting groups in technology adoption decision-making or from installing or optimizing technology solutions to building online degree programs. Positions require strong skills in patience and problem-solving, proficiency in using a variety of technology tools, and communicating equally well with technology experts and novices.

Enrollment Services Positions

Enrollment services positions include domestic and international student recruiters, admissions readers, and enrollment or admissions consultants. Entry-level work involves tasks such as evaluating admissions requirements for undergraduate and/or graduate students, giving presentations, representing an institution at recruitment events, and coordinating recruitment activities and/or admission events. Positions require abilities such as managing multiple assignments accurately, communicating in multiple formats and environments, having interpersonal skills, and using databases and other enrollment technologies.

Business Development and Advancement Positions

Development and advancement positions include budget planning consultants, fund-raisers, and donor outreach consultants. Entry-level work involves knowing an institution well; being able to convey its mission, values, achievements, and goals in conversations and writing; organizing fund-raising activities; providing policy or program analyses for complex philanthropic gifts; and creating tools and templates for advancement projects. Positions require skills such as writing and communication, organization, interpersonal relations, analysis and problem-solving, and creativity.

Marketing and Communications Positions

Marketing and communications positions include public relations staff, social media coordinators, online community managers, content producers, writers, and editors. Entry-level work entails tasks such as researching marketing trends in higher education; contributing to or creating marketing plans and campaigns; working with website, social media, print, and direct mail technologies; and communicating internally to an institution's community and externally to outside influencer audiences or potential students. Positions require abilities such as communicating well, using marketing technologies proficiently, conceptualizing and/or executing marketing content and campaigns, and conducting and analyzing marketing surveys.

Campus Administration Positions

Campus administration positions include compensation specialists, human resources operations, procurement directors or staff, and interim administrators (e.g., during searches). Entry-level work may entail coordinating personnel recruitment, interviewing, and hiring; managing an employee database, payroll, and absence management systems; supporting procurement projects; and analyzing contracts. Positions require strong skills in communication, analysis, relationship-building, and organization.

Accreditation Support Positions

Accreditation support positions include accreditation preparation and remediation consultants. Entry-level work involves tasks such as auditing and preparing an institution's portfolio of evidence for internal or external accreditation review, training an institution's accreditation committee or team in navigating the accreditation process, and supporting an institution as it responds to reviewer feedback. Positions require strong organizational, interpersonal, and analytical skills and attention to detail.

Project Management Positions
Project management positions include building construction or retrofit managers and space planning consultants. Entry-level work entails sending and managing project communications, coordinating project budget and task lists, tracking and reporting project progress, and scheduling project meetings. Positions require the ability to keep stakeholders focused on project goals and scope, gather and synthesize organizational knowledge, identify and sequence tasks, manage risk, and communicate effectively.

Next Steps

If one of the job categories or example positions in this chapter sounds interesting to you, but you want more information, then there are a number of actions you can take. You can review job descriptions for similar positions by searching a website dedicated to jobs in higher education. On HigherEdJobs.com you can filter your searches by category such as administrative, faculty, or executive; location; type of school; and type of job, for example, remote, dual career, or adjunct. *Inside Higher Ed* (careers.inside highered.com) provides tabs for faculty jobs and administrative jobs in units like academic affairs, business affairs, technology, and student affairs.

The Higher Education Recruitment Consortium (HERC; www.hercjobs .org) allows you to filter jobs by type, including adjunct and non-tenure-track; postdoc, internship, and fellowship; temporary or per diem; and even online or remote positions. The HERC jobs search tool also allows you to create job alerts where you set your criteria and get an e-mail each time campuses post new jobs that match them. Another next step might be to conduct informational interviews with people who work in the roles you may want to fill. For more details, see Part Three, where you'll learn about alt-ac fields through informational interviews, job shadowing, and more.

4

ALT-AC OPPORTUNITIES OUTSIDE ACADEMIA

In this chapter, you will (a) consider in more detail alt-ac careers outside higher education institutions, such as research, education policy, and educational technology, and (b) explore questions designed to determine if this is the right career path for you.

Alt-Ac Positions Beyond the Campus

While many alt-ac positions can be found at higher education institutions, they can also be found beyond the campus. A number of organizations serve the higher education sector, have their own academically oriented missions, or both. These organizations may be for-profit or non-profit, private or governmental. This alt-ac work includes job categories in a variety of areas outside academic institutions, including, but not limited to, publishing and content development, industry research and development, student support, public service, educational technology and software development, nonprofit work, cultural and historical organizations, business and finance, and consulting and entrepreneurship.

Publishing and Content Development

If you have written or will be writing a dissertation or thesis, then you may have already considered turning your work into published articles or a book. Given the time and effort that you devoted to studying a topic and writing up your findings, it makes good sense to share your ideas in as many formats as possible (for more details, see chapter 17, "Making Good Use of a Dissertation After Graduation," and chapter 22, "Writing and Publishing").

Extrapolating further, another way to translate your unique combination of discipline expertise and writing experience is to pursue a publishing and content development position (e.g., literary agent or editor) or a position supporting marketing, sales, or production. Textbooks are published every year by traditional, for-profit publishers (e.g., Wiley, McGraw-Hill, Pearson, Cengage), as well as an increasing number of organizations dedicated to creating high-quality, open textbooks (e.g., OER Commons, Open Access Textbooks, Community College Consortium for Open Educational Resources). Along with those textbooks, many publishers and open educational resource developers create ancillary instructional materials, such as lecture presentations, learning objects, test banks, and educational multimedia.

Brad Franklin's first love in learning was mathematics, which—coupled with an early interest in computing—led to a decade of mathematics research and teaching in the Big 10 and a PhD along the way. As he transformed his own classroom by developing web assessments and online learning experiences, he became a resource for science faculty members at the University of Nebraska–Lincoln, where he took on an instructional-design-and-technology role. This led to 15 years in learning technologies and product-design manager positions at Wiley Publishing, where he managed and provided support, training, and professional development to tens of thousands of other math, science, accounting, and engineering faculty members.

After a mid-career break spent homeschooling, he's returning to the classroom as a science, technology, engineering, and mathematics (STEM) program director at Hebrew Academy of Long Beach, where he is establishing an engineering design curriculum and experience for middle school students. Teaching his own children and their peers has reignited his passion for education:

> I am excited to share the beauty and utility of mathematics and the power of the engineering design process in a supportive, learner-centered environment to position students for success in their lives and careers. In all of my endeavors—teaching online, course development, faculty training, market development, product design, customer success, and Customer Relationship Management (CRM) development—I focus on identifying opportunities (aka "problems"), developing solutions, optimizing workflows, and creating content and experiences to help both customers and colleagues to succeed. While I have a strong computational background and use coding to automate a wide range of technologies, my success has come from employing the "low-tech" but high-leverage traits of empathy and integrity. (B. Franklin, personal communication, July 1, 2019)

Student Support

If you have experience as a tutor, coach, counselor, or academic adviser, then you might consider a student support role, such as a leadership or staff position for a private tutoring center or online tutoring service or an independent contractor working through a tutoring platform. Large higher education publishers hire people in a variety of disciplines to provide tutoring as an additional service to subscribing colleges and universities. For example, Pearson acquired the online tutoring service Smarthinking and offers college-level tutoring support in the following fields: business, career writing, computers and technology, math and statistics, nursing and allied health, reading, science, Spanish, and writing.

Higher education institutions also contract with organizations like NetTutor and Upswing that combine different aspects of student support like advising, tutoring, and mentoring. These companies hire tutors and coaches, as well as more permanent and senior roles in areas like sales (e.g., to manage accounts) and technology (e.g., to develop and improve student retention software platforms).

Other organizations like UniversityTutor connect students with tutors in their geographic area. Tutors on the UniversityTutor site set their own fees—between $10 and $250 per hour—and keep 100% of what they earn. Ratings and reviews can lead to more clients and credibility that merit rate increases.

Technology and Software

The educational technology and software industry has been growing exponentially, and whether or not you have a computer science background, this industry offers opportunities to programmers and subject matter experts alike. If you have both disciplinary expertise and programming experience, that is even better. Technology and software roles include learning content developers, online course developers and facilitators, educational software and app developers, instructional designers, multimedia project managers, production managers, and technical writers.

The organizations hiring for these positions range from large higher education publishers to small start-ups. There are other technology and software positions related to specific disciplines, too. For example, new technologies emerge every day to support fast-growing industries like biochemistry or solar energy. You can find educational technology jobs at large job sites (e.g., Indeed.com or Monster.com) or sites that specialize in the field (e.g., educationaltechnology.net).

After 25 years of teaching physics at Swarthmore College, Carl Grossman took an extended leave of absence to apply his science skills beyond the campus borders. He worked with TeachSpin, a New York company that creates instruments designed for teaching physics and engineering topics through hands-on activities. Then he joined Brava Home, a California-based start-up company, as the director of science and research. He may go back to a university someday, but he is enjoying using his physics knowledge and skills to develop real-world, practical solutions in his current alt-ac role.

Nonprofit Organizations and Professional Associations

If you have a degree related to policy or public administration, experience writing grants, or a cause for which you want to do more than donate time or money, then you may want to explore a role at a nonprofit organization. Positions at nonprofits include organizational leaders, policy analysts and developers, fund-raisers and grant writers, program developers and evaluators, and researchers. In some cases, your research may lead you to create a nonprofit organization from the ground up.

Did you join any professional organizations or discipline-based associations during or after your graduate studies? Association positions cover a spectrum, starting with unpaid roles that require only a small investment of time, such as advisory board members; moving to temporary, project-based positions, such as consultants; and ending with permanent, salaried staff and administrator roles in areas such as outreach or membership coordination, strategic planning, and operations.

Government Agencies

Are you called to serve your country and want to know about options beyond the military? Government and public service roles include those you might expect, such as federal, state, and local government agency directors and staff; policy analysts; and public relations staff. Positions you might not expect include engineers, statisticians, computer scientists, chemists, economists, information technology managers, business and finance professionals (e.g., auditing, contracting), and public health professionals. If any of these positions interest you, it is easy to search for available positions in the U.S. and Canadian governments or in another country of your choice.

The U.S. government jobs site (www.USAjobs.gov) identifies the most urgent hiring needs by field ("Explore Opportunities" tab) and allows you to create a profile to support your application ("Create a USAJOBS Profile" tab). The Canadian government jobs site (www.jobbank.gc.ca) allows you to match jobs and career options based on your skills and knowledge, as well as your fields of study. If you are interested in working in another country, there may be similar job websites that you can peruse for possible career opportunities.

Cultural Organizations

Did your graduate studies focus on some aspect of culture, and you want to continue working in a related area? Positions at cultural organizations include administrators and staff at museums or cultural centers, ethnomusicologists, fund-raisers and grant writers, program and curriculum developers, and community outreach staff. You can find more than 500 different job banks for employment opportunities at cultural organizations through the Cultural Jobs site (www.culturaljobs.org).

Search the job banks to find the few that serve your field of interest, such as art; anthropology; theater, music, and dance; museums, cultural centers, and public gardens; and much more. For example, if you have a degree in museum studies, then visit the American Alliance of Museums, which maintains a "Careers and JobHQ" site (www.aam-us.org/resources/careers) that has a job search engine and a link to start building your professional network.

Research Institutes and Labs

Have you enjoyed your doctoral research experience and want to continue working in an industry research and development position? Private institutes and companies offer a variety of research opportunities, including roles like scientists and engineers, science communicators, decision scientists, market analysts, product managers, and policy developers. The research conducted by these organizations often moves an industry forward through discoveries and innovations.

For example, SRI International (www.sri.com) is a well-known research institute that serves a number of sectors, including biosciences and health systems, energy, computing and technology, defense and security, education and learning, ocean and space, and robotics. For almost 50 years the Palo Alto Research Center (www.parc.com), formerly known as Xerox PARC, has been responsible for major developments in personal computing, printable electronics, data and image analytics, and much more.

Some research institutes focus on one field; for instance, the nonprofit Scripps Research Institute (www.scripps.edu) exclusively does research in biomedical science and since 1980 has created over 70 spin-off companies. Medical and health research institutes hire chemists, immunologists, microbiologists, neuroscientists, medical communication specialists, health-care information technology specialists, quantitative analysts, and medical science liaisons. Other professional research positions include research directors and foundation grant reviewers. You can find a comprehensive list of medical research institutes in the United States on Wikipedia (en.wikipedia.org/wiki/Category:Medical_research_institutes_in_the_United_States). From this page you can investigate institutes that are located in your geographic area, focused on your area of discipline expertise, and advertising open positions.

Companies and Start-Ups

Is your doctoral degree in a field related to business? Have you earned a master of business administration (MBA) degree as a terminal degree or in addition to a doctorate or other terminal degree? Alt-ac roles in business and finance include operations research analysts, market research analysts, sales managers, business development managers, competitive intelligence analysts, product managers, and management consultants. Entrepreneurial alt-ac roles include start-up cofounders or leaders, product developers, and marketing staff. To get an idea about the new start-ups that are emerging in your field, take a look at 500 Startups and sort by market (500.co/startups) or go to the Startups List and look for start-ups in a particular city near you (startups-list.com).

Consulting Firms

Are you interested in striking out on your own as a higher education consultant or joining a consulting firm? Alt-ac consulting positions may be related to your specific discipline, organizational development, business analysis, professional development, academic technology, distance education or online program management, or instructional design. We cover consulting work in more detail in Part Five, but you may want to begin thinking about the possibilities. To explore the types of consulting work taking place today, take a look at websites for

- big consulting firms that have higher education expertise as part of their overall offer, like Huron Consulting Group's Higher Education unit (www.huronconsultinggroup.com/self-id/higher-education) and Deloitte's Higher Education Services (www2.deloitte.com/us/en/pages/public-sector/solutions/higher-education-services.html);

- smaller consulting firms that specialize in serving higher education, like Credo (www.credohighered.com) and Kennedy & Company (kennedyandcompany.com); or
- individual higher education consultants like Thomas J. Tobin (thomas jtobin.com) and Kathryn E. Linder (drkatielinder.com).

As you review these sites and others like them, make a note of any specialties or consulting areas that you want to pursue.

Next Steps

If one of the job categories or example positions in this chapter sounds interesting to you, and you want more information, you can learn more by reviewing job descriptions for similar positions on websites that list "jobs outside academe" or "jobs outside higher education." Here are just a few examples:

- Chronicle Vitae's job search (chroniclevitae.com/job_search) has a filter for jobs outside academe that includes nonprofit and government organizations, educational organizations, and for-profit organizations.
- The HERC site we shared in the previous chapter (www.hercjobs .org) allows you to search by organization types beyond higher education institutions, including business and industry, government agencies, hospitals, nonprofits and associations, research institutes and labs, and other education or health-care organizations.
- *Inside Higher Ed* (careers.insidehighered.com) provides a tab to browse jobs outside of higher education, such as businesses and consultancies, government agencies, museums and cultural organizations, nonprofits, public policy, publishers and presses, research and development, software and technology, and more.
- Columbia University's Center for Career Education (www.career .columbia.edu/resources/non-academic-career-options-phds-humanities-and-social-sciences) shares resources for alt-ac careers for people with PhD degrees in the humanities and social sciences. The site has examples and links to additional information for job categories including consulting, nonprofits, financial services, K–12 teaching, publishing, cultural and historical organizations, U.S. government, professional research, international development, and entrepreneurship.

5

BEING AWARE OF EMOTIONS WHEN MAKING CAREER DECISIONS

In this chapter, you will (a) address the potential emotional aspects of making the decision to pursue an alt-ac career, (b) determine if and how often you will revisit your decision, and (c) gain strategies to address emotions.

Check In With Yourself and Check Up on Your Emotions

If you are familiar with needs assessment work, then you know the process basically boils down to answering three questions: Where are you now? Where do you want to be? How do you get there? The first question—Where are you now?—is usually the easiest to answer, as you can assess what you are doing right now. It may take some scrutiny and work, but it can be done by listing your current status in different aspects of your life: personal, professional, social, creative, and so on. With respect to your career, you can simply point to where you currently find yourself in the alt-ac career space (see Figure 1.1). The second question—Where do you want to be?—can be harder to answer because it involves not only your goals but also your dreams. Dreams are ethereal. Dreams can be emotional. To get a better picture of how this applies to making decisions about your career, let's conduct an emotional assessment before we address the third question—How do you get there?

Basic Emotions

Start with a simple self-check of two basic emotions, *happiness* and *sadness*. How are you feeling right now? Rate your happiness on a scale of 0 (*none*) to 5 (*very happy*). Also rate your sadness on a scale of 0 (*none*) to 5 (*very sad*). While these emotions are opposites, these are two separate scales, so you can be a little (or a lot) of both. For each emotion, try to determine why you might be feeling that way at this moment. For example, you might feel happy that you are close to earning your degree, while you might feel slightly sad that you will not see some of your classmates after graduating. If you have already earned your degree, you might feel happy about making a discovery during your postdoctoral work but feel sad that your adjunct teaching position was not renewed this semester. When you are making decisions, it is useful to check your mood regularly, to track changes in mood over time and to identify potential underlying causes.

Emotions Related to a Real or an Imagined Position

In a review of different theories about emotion, David Robinson (2008) outlined contrasting emotions related to objects, events, ourselves, others, and even the future. For our purposes, we will look at emotions related to an "object," which we will interpret as a current or potential job. Flip back to Figure 1.1 again, which depicts a variety of careers—academic, alt-ac, and non-ac. What emotions emerge when you look at your current position or possible future jobs? Rate your *attraction* to specific jobs on a scale of 0 (*none*) to 5 (*very attracted*). Similarly, rate your *aversion* to each job on a scale of 0 (*none*) to 5 (*very averse*). If attraction and aversion are not the correct contrast pair, then try rating your *interest*—also associated with enthusiasm and curiosity—and *indifference*—sometimes characterized by boredom or accommodation (Robinson, 2008). Determining these emotions may help you plot your career path.

Emotions Related to Events

As you travel along your career path, you will have feelings about your current status or emotional responses to specific events, especially when your current or perceived progress toward an outcome seems beyond your control. Assess what emotions you feel when (a) you consider where you are right now, professionally, and (b) something happens that affects you and your career. The contrasting emotion pairs related to events are *gratitude* and *anger*, *joy* and *sorrow*, *patience* and *frustration*, and *contentment* and *discontentment* (Robinson, 2008). Pick the scales that make the most sense, or use them all! For example, rate your patience with respect to your progress toward your career goals on a scale of 0 (*none*) to 5 (*very patient*). On the flip side, rate your frustration with respect to that same progress on a scale of 0 (*none*) to 5 (*very frustrated*). Restlessness may also be an indicator of frustration.

Emotions Related to the Future

The last set of emotions we will explore in this chapter relates to the future, or our perceptions of our own future. Robinson (2008) described *hope* and *fear* as the two contrasting emotions that tell us how we feel about what might come next. Rate how you feel about your future career on both scales, from 0 (*none*) to 5 (*very hopeful* or *very fearful*).

Make Decisions in Light of—or in Spite of—Emotions

Now that you have checked in with yourself and a few of your emotions, you can focus on how they might affect your decisions and take steps to address their impact. As we suggested earlier in this chapter, you will also want to perform a brief assessment of your emotions on a regular basis—from once a month to once or twice a year—so you are aware of how your feelings change over time. Research studies have found that some emotions like fear, anger, or sadness affect our ability to make decisions in general (e.g., Ma-Kellams & Lerner, 2016), while knowing and being able to manage one's emotional state can improve career adaptability (e.g., Coetzee & Harry, 2014).

A consistently high rating of frustration—for example, the constant ambiguity of not yet having a concrete career goal—can create an emotional tension that builds over time. Furthermore, it can lead to crescendo-like moments when you feel like you have to make career decisions for fundamental reasons like paying your rent or mortgage. Later, you may end up feeling that making career decisions for those reasons will keep you from discovering your calling. After all, in Maslow's hierarchy of needs, physiological needs like food and shelter come first, well before self-actualization (Maslow, 1943).

A permanent or temporary departure from your chosen path—for example, the inability to find a specific alt-ac or tenure-track position several months after you graduate or complete your postdoctoral work—can seem like the death of a dream. A high rating of sorrow may lead to behaviors described as the five stages of grief—denial, anger, depression, bargaining, and acceptance—that Elisabeth Kübler-Ross (1969) first introduced. The death of a dream may be prevented given enough time, especially if you are able to make some changes or if external conditions change in your favor. If not, the grieving period may just lead to the birth of a new dream.

In this competitive higher education job market, we recommend that you avoid taking a passive, wait-and-see approach. Instead, consider creating a plan to assess your situation after six months or a year. Identify short-term goals that improve the chances for you to realize your initial dream, your new dream, or both. Publish articles based on your dissertation research. Select an alt-ac position that sets you up to gain valuable skills.

For example, working in an educational development capacity allows you to study evidence-based teaching techniques that increase student success. Working for a research institution that has a postdoctoral position opening in your time frame might allow you to get experience setting up a lab, working with data, writing grant proposals and evaluations, and more. If you still have not determined your ultimate career goal, then pursuing alt-ac positions can give you options down the road.

If you have been living in the culture of academia for any length of time, people have probably asked you questions like "What's your major?" or "What do you want to be?" Rather than associating our future identity with a specific role like a professor, we might better frame the situation through new questions such as "What problems do you want to solve?" This new question works well for our needs assessment too.

A Note About Dreams

If you have decided to pursue a specific alt-ac career as your new dream, take time to grieve the death of your original dream—such as a different alt-ac position or the tenure track—and find closure. More often than not, this is a difficult process. Leigh Cousins (2011) from *Psych Central* tells us why it can be so difficult:

> Our dreams exist, *for real*, in our brain's circuitry. An important dream is built up through lots of repetitions of a cherished idea, which makes for very strong and sturdy neural connections.
>
> Those connections don't then easily disconnect as soon as we realize that our dream won't come true. The disconnection and rerouting process is long and painful. (para. 5–6)

After reading Sheryl Sandberg's (2017) book *Option B: Facing Adversity, Building Resilience, and Finding Joy*, grief educators Litsa Williams and Eleanor Haley (2018) described the importance of mourning the loss of a dream:

> We have choices to make. We could hold on tight and keep carrying our hopes and dreams forward, but such a heavy and hollow load limits our capacity to find other more fulfilling alternatives. We could drop everything and walk around angry and bitter, but this distracts us from finding joy in the things we do have and leaves our arms empty. Or finally, we could find ways to grieve our losses and someday, if we're lucky, we'll gain enough peace and acceptance to embrace our option B. (para. 11)

Embracing our option B is the starting point for Brett Fox (2015), a career coach who also prescribed "giving yourself time to grieve" (para. 23). He then outlined the following seemingly simple steps to realize new dreams: (a) maintain a positive and open mind-set, (b) visualize what you want, (c) keep track of your ideas, and (d) take action (Fox, 2015). Holding up a notable, historical figure as a model, Fox recalled that Abraham Lincoln "went through five different careers before he found his calling" (para. 49). In other words, you can do this!

Next Steps

Regardless of where you are in your journey, one thing you can do is your own needs assessment. Remember the three questions: Where are you now? Where do you want to be, or what problems do you want to solve? How do you get there? List the action items you need to complete to achieve your current career goal. If you are still completing your graduate degree, then an early action item might be to learn more about alt-ac fields through informational interviews (more on this later in this book). If you have recently completed your graduate degree, then your list will include mapping a career trajectory, which you will do in the next chapter. If you have decided to leave the tenure track for an alt-ac career, then your list will include identifying transferrable skills, a task you will complete in chapter 16. In all three cases, one of your action items will be finding the right alt-ac position for you. Part Three of our book provides practical steps for getting started.

6

MAPPING AN ALT-AC
CAREER TRAJECTORY

In this chapter, you will (a) project possible career paths that align with your interests and your graduate work and (b) consider professional milestones, life events, and other decisions that affect progress along these pathways.

Choosing Your Own Adventure

If you have been planning for most of your career to be in a tenure-track role, then you've had the good fortune of a career trajectory already mapped out for you. After landing the elusive tenure-track position, you would work for six or seven years to achieve tenure, possibly with a three-year review along the way. This would involve building on a lot of the skills that you were introduced to in graduate school: teaching, scholarship, and service. Depending on your institution, certain of these skills might be prioritized over others.

Upon earning tenure (hooray!), you would then work for the next milestone of associate professor, followed by promotion to full professor. While we certainly would not argue that this path is easy, we do think that it's pretty well laid out. There are also lots of resources to help you navigate this more traditional tenure-track path (e.g., see Goldsmith, Komlos, & Schine Gold, 2010; Gray & Drew, 2012; Haviland, Ortiz, & Henriques, 2017). Even if you start out looking for (or even getting) a tenure-track faculty position, many things can change your career arc (e.g., life circumstances, not being awarded tenure). This book can help you keep your options open; see especially chapter 12 on collecting and preparing alt-ac materials.

Alt-ac career paths are a little more of a choose-your-own-adventure set of options. Once you enter into an alt-ac role, you may decide to work your way up through a series of promotions at your university or company. You may also decide to work in one area for a while before shifting to a different unit or department once you have developed some new skills. Your alt-ac career trajectory is, in some ways, entirely up to you. We recommend trying to create a multiyear plan for your alt-ac career trajectory so that you can plan your next steps even as you are working in your current position. The following activities can help you decide some of the stops along the way of your career map, but keep in mind that those stops are flexible and can (and will) change over time.

Creating a Multiyear Career Map

For some people a multiyear career plan can seem overwhelming, but consider that all tenure-track jobs come with these multiyear plans built in—we're just mapping a different pathway. As you begin to think about your multiyear career map, you don't need to worry about the timing piece quite yet. Instead, we recommend thinking about the different stops—personal and professional—that you are intending to include on your larger career map. Here are some guiding questions to help you get started.

Personal Stops on Your Map

- What are the major familial milestones that you see occurring for you in the next 5 to 10 years?
- What are the major financial milestones that you see occurring for you in the next 5 to 10 years?
- What are the major health and wellness milestones that you see occurring for you in the next 5 to 10 years?
- What are the major personal development milestones that you see occurring for you in the next 5 to 10 years?

Professional Stops on Your Map

- Can you currently identify any small or large milestones along your alt-ac career path? (Keep in mind that these can be a future vision rather than a concrete reality at this point—feel free to dream big!)
- Do you want to teach, train, or facilitate learning for others throughout your career? What might this look like in your ideal scenario?
- Do you want to write and publish things throughout your career? What kinds of things do you most want to write and publish? (Think broadly here—blog posts, poetry, and recipes can count just as much as articles, grants, and books.)

- Do you want to supervise others throughout your career? If yes, what size team do you envision supervising 5 to 10 years from now?
- Do you anticipate needing to develop significantly different skill sets or abilities than what you can currently do to achieve certain milestones along your career path?
- What are your financial goals for your career? Can you identify particular milestones of when you hope to achieve certain financial goals?

Answering each of these questions may cause you to ask yourself *even more* questions about what your future career path might include. That's okay! Mapping out an alt-ac choose-your-own-adventure pathway sometimes means having more questions than answers. In the next section, we provide a sample career map matrix so that you can see how it might look to map out your answers to the previous questions.

Sample Career Mapping Matrix

As you start to think about the major milestones along your alt-ac career pathway, we recommend writing them down. This can not only serve as an actual guide as you progress throughout your career but also allow you to see when the map needs to be changed or adjusted along the way. Career maps also allow you to set goals for yourself regarding areas or issues you want to learn more about. This allows you to have those ideas top of mind as new opportunities are presented to you throughout your career. Table 6.1 provides an example career map from Linder's five-year plan from her first alt-ac job out of graduate school. She completed the Learn and Do columns first to project everything she wanted to accomplish professionally, and then she filled in the Milestones column later to show what she achieved.

The career map in Table 6.1 is set up with the simple categories of the year, followed by areas for what to learn and do, with a final column to mark the accomplishments from that year. This example illustrates how career maps can be future-oriented documents while they can also be a tool for keeping a record over one's career milestones over time. Keep in mind that you can map out your multiyear pathway in whatever way is helpful to you. You can choose your own categories to build a personalized map.

Your Future Curriculum Vitae or Résumé

In some ways, you can think about the career map matrix as a more visual version of your *curriculum vitae* (CV) or résumé (see chapter 12 for more information on the differences between the two documents). Another way of mapping

TABLE 6.1
Sample Multiyear Career Map

Years	Learn	Do	Milestones
2010–2011	Settle into new job and read more about consultation and workshop facilitation	Publish seminar papers from graduate courses	Promoted from assistant to associate director; published four articles from graduate school
2011–2012	Learn more about grant writing and managing other people	Write and publish first article in faculty development	Promoted from associate director to director; began managing staff
2012–2013	Learn about book proposals	Write grant to support faculty development programs; write book proposal and secure contract for first book; start mapping second book	Received first grant to support faculty development programs; submitted first book proposal and signed contract
2013–2014	Read about keynoting and public speaking; complete leadership in higher education professional development program	Write larger grant to support faculty development programs; get contract for second book	Applied for and received first grant to conduct research; received third grant to support collaborative grant with other campuses; first book published; started to keynote and speak at other campuses; hired additional staff
2014–2015	Read about research methods, particularly quantitative methods using statistics	Go on the market for my next job (position TBD)	Contract received for second book

your career for those who are more linear thinkers is to think about what your CV or résumé will contain in 5 to 10 years. This exercise can be a fun way of imagining what you hope you will achieve in your career that would be important enough to add to a CV or résumé for sharing with others.

For example, what courses do you hope to teach? What kinds of position titles do you want to hold? What size of budgets do you want to manage? What skills do you want to grow or enhance? What conferences do you want to present at? What additional education (either formal or informal) do you want to pursue? What audiences do you want to influence? What books do you want to publish and with which publishers? In short, what kind of impact do you want to have on the world? Building a future CV or résumé is another way of logging your goals for an alt-ac career pathway so that you can work toward specific milestones and areas of learning as you progress throughout your career.

Alternative Planning Strategies

For those of you who have read about the previous exercises and felt a bit lost, never fear. We know that multiyear career mapping does not work for everyone, particularly if you are early in your alt-ac career and don't know quite what you want to do yet. We have all been at a similar point in our careers when we were not sure what our next step would be. Here are some strategies if you are feeling a little lacking in the direction department.

Identify the Things That You Like to Do
If you are just getting started with trying to figure out your alt-ac career pathway, identifying the things you like to do is a fine starting point. One way of identifying your professional sweet spot is to think about those times when you achieve what Csikszentmihalyi (2009) called *flow,* or those areas of your professional life where you tend to lose track of time, forget to eat, and just fall into the work. Some people achieve a flow state in writing, others in running or physical activity, still others in creating art. A flow state is a good sign that you are doing something you like and are passionate about.

Look for the Gaps and Trends
Newport (2012) argued against the career advice of just following your passion; in his book *So Good They Can't Ignore You,* he provided examples of how skills trump passion in the professional world. Although we definitely think you should do work that you enjoy, we tend to agree about the importance of developing skills, especially for alt-ac roles. If you are not sure what to do

next, learn next, or devote your professional energy to, look around to see the areas that seem to always be in demand. (See chapter 15, "Finding a Niche and an Appropriate Audience," for more about finding gaps.) In the higher education world, for example, data analysis is becoming a hot new trend. If you happen to enjoy crunching numbers, you probably won't need to worry about job security if you were to move in this direction.

Learn Some New Skills
Seeking out the gaps in your field or career area of choice might mean needing to pick up some new skills. If you are just out of graduate school, becoming a student again might not be the most attractive idea for you, but if you are in mid-career and hoping to start or continue in an alt-ac career, going back to school (literally or figuratively) might be just what you need. Consider taking a course or training (massive open online courses [MOOCs] can be great for professional learners), reading books or articles in a new area of interest, or listening to podcast episodes that address a field you want to learn more about.

Next Steps

If you are still a bit concerned about what direction to go in, take a look at Wapnick's (2017) *How to Be Everything*, a career guide for what Wapnick calls *multipotentialites*, or those people who just aren't sure what to do with the rest of their lives. Multipotentialites are known for pursuing lots of different kinds of professional areas, switching careers several times throughout their lives, and juggling lots of projects at once. Sound familiar? Check out Wapnick's books for career strategies and tips if you like to do lots of things at once or get bored easily.

If you are a little surer about your direction, take your career map to the next level. Grab a large piece of poster board, some sticky notes and colored markers, and go to town. Many people have discussed the benefits of having a vision board, and your career map can serve the same purpose. An additional tool to explore is the Career Exploration Road Map (mind.ucsf.edu/article/mind-career-exploration-road-map) available from the University of California, San Francisco, which offers a visual way to reflect on different career options. Get creative with how you want to visually represent your next five years so that you have something that you enjoy revisiting. When you are done, hang your career map in a place of prominence so that you can review it whenever is useful to you. We all believe in the magic of writing goals down to make sure they stay top of mind, so use this activity as a way to get creative while you create space for your professional aspirations.

7

LEARNING MORE ABOUT ALT-AC FIELDS

In this chapter, you will review (a) the information that can be gained from connecting with current alt-ac professionals and (b) strategies for connecting with others in alt-ac positions.

No Two Alt-Ac Stories Are the Same

As you start to learn more about different alt-ac positions, one thing you will find is the wide range of alt-ac career trajectories. People transition into alt-ac roles from a diverse set of disciplines and at different career stages. No two stories will be the same. For this reason, talking with people who are in alt-ac positions about how they came to be in those roles can be incredibly useful.

While you probably will not be able to follow their exact plan for landing their particular alt-ac job, you will be able to see the kinds of skills they developed, the network they created, and the opportunities they leveraged to get themselves into their current career pathway. In this chapter, we'll explore some of the key ways to learn from current alt-ac job holders such as informational interviews, job shadowing, and internships.

Informational Interviews

Informational interviews are intentional conversations that help the interviewer learn more about a particular job or career pathway. These conversations can happen with colleagues you know or colleagues you do not know but contact just for this purpose. Each of us authoring this book has had experiences of being contacted for informational interviews from people we do not know well, especially contacts we have made through social media, and each of us has been happy to engage in these conversations about our current roles and pathways. Here are some strategies for finding potential informational interviewees:

- Review the recent alumni job placements in your current department.
- Search key words on professional networking platforms such as LinkedIn, Academia.edu, and ResearchGate.
- Ask friends and colleagues for their contacts in specific career areas of interest to you.
- Read recent research coming out of the career area of interest to you and note authors who may be useful contacts.
- Explore key voices in your field of interest who are actively engaged on social media platforms such as LinkedIn, Twitter, or Facebook.
- Talk to people at career fairs and events organized by campus career centers.
- Read through academic blogs of people in your career area of interest; many people are now sharing about their career pathways via blogging.

Once you have gathered a potential list of informational interview contacts, you will want to reach out and see if they are willing to speak to you. We have included a sample e-mail template that has worked for us (see Box 7.1).

Although not everyone whom you contact will be willing to speak with you, many people are willing to have a conversation with a junior colleague to share their experience, especially if that conversation is brief. Another possibility is to offer to take the interviewee to coffee or out to lunch as an incentive to chat with you.

BOX 7.1.
Informational Interview Invitation E-Mail Template

Dear Dr. [person's last name],

I am exploring a potential career in [career area]. I found your work through [search technique] and was hoping to talk to you for about 20 minutes or so about your career pathway and any resources you have found useful along the way. Here are some dates and times that I would be available for a quick call:

- Date and time #1 [note time zone of interviewee]
- Date and time #2 [note time zone of interviewee]
- Date and time #3 [note time zone of interviewee]

Thanks for your consideration. I would love to learn from your experience
Sincerely,
Your name

Here are some potential questions that might be useful to get the conversation started once you have the informational interview scheduled:

- What pathway led to your current position?
- How did you know that you wanted to pursue your current career?
- What is surprising to you about your current role?
- What are your favorite and least favorite parts of your current role?
- What advice do you have for someone who wants to enter your field?
- Are there any resources that were particularly helpful for you?

There are certainly questions you can add to this list, but remember that you want to keep the conversation as short as you originally promised to be respectful of your interviewee's time.

As you interview different people in your career area(s) of interest, you may start to see overlaps in the following:

- Recommended skills to develop
- Training opportunities
- Important resources or advice

Pay attention to and take notes capturing the information you receive from multiple interviewees, because those may be particularly useful focus areas for you to dedicate time and energy to as you pursue your alt-ac role.

Indirect Informational Interviews

If contacting strangers to set up personal conversations is not your cup of tea, we have some other methods of gathering information about alt-ac roles. There are several resources where people are discussing their alt-ac careers and where you can lurk in a more anonymous way. Think of the following methods as covert informational interviews.

The You've Got This *Podcast*

The *You've Got This* podcast (drkatielinder.com/ygt) is a weekly show for academics and higher education professionals interested in productivity and surviving and thriving in the day to day of academic life. Hosted by Linder, the show frequently offers glimpses into the alt-ac life, especially in relation to speaking, consulting, and authoring books outside of a traditional faculty position.

The Make Your Way *Podcast*

The *Make Your Way* podcast (drkatielinder.com/ygt) is a resource for academic creatives, freelancers, and entrepreneurs who are small business owners or who have aspirations to build their own businesses. Cohosted by Linder and Sara Langworthy, this podcast goes deep into what it means to be alt-ac from the perspective of someone working in academia full-time while nurturing a side business and someone who has left academia altogether to pursue her own business full-time.

The Wealthy Teachers *Podcast*

The *Wealthy Teachers* podcast is an interview-based podcast (https://podcasts.apple.com/us/podcast/wealthyteachers/id1330333131) hosted by Lindsay Padilla where she chats with academics who have transitioned to self-employment or who are pursuing "side gigs" while also engaging in full-time academic positions. Padilla's guests represent a range of disciplinary backgrounds and industries.

Beyond the Professoriate

An online community for academics and higher education professionals working outside of the typical tenure track, Beyond the Professoriate (community.beyondprof.com) includes a library of video interviews, live workshops and conference sessions, and individual and group coaching specifically related to alt-ac careers.

Post-PhD Online Interviews

There are a surprising number of bloggers interviewing academics post-PhD who have pursued alt-ac roles. Here are a few to get you started:

- Humanists at Work (humwork.uchri.org): Check out their "stories from the field" video series.
- The Versatile PhD (versatilephd.com): Check to see if your institution is a subscribing member.
- PhDs at Work (phdsatwork.com): Check out the "Week in the Life" section.
- From PhD to Life (fromphdtolife.com): Check out the Transition Q&As posted to the blog.
- Beyond the PhD (beyondthephd.co.uk): Check out the profiles section.
- Vitae (www.vitae.ac.uk): Check out the careers section in particular.

All of the resources described here can help you learn more about alt-ac roles and positions without leaving your computer.

Job Shadowing

Job shadowing is another excellent way to learn more about a person's career path and to explore whether a particular kind of alt-ac job might be a good fit for you. Job shadowing can be a short-term or a long-term time investment, depending on the situation. Short-term job shadows might take just one day, with you accompanying a colleague to various meetings and activities with a short debrief at the end of your time together to ask questions about what you have experienced. These short-term job shadows may be most convenient if they are located within a short geographical distance of where you live, but they can also be coordinated with conference travel or a short visit to another city if there is a specific person you are hoping to shadow.

Longer term job shadowing is meant to help you experience a particular position more fully by participating in activities related to that position over a longer period of time. This deeper level of job shadowing might entail multiple visits over time; for example, once a month for a semester. You will see greater benefit if you take the time to reflect on each recent shadowing experience and prepare for each upcoming shadowing experience as you go. Some internships act as longer term job shadowing roles. Another good example of this kind of role is placements made through the American Council on Education Fellows Program (www.acenet.edu/leadership/programs/Pages/ACE-Fellows-Program.aspx) or through the Professional and Organizational Development (POD) Network Diversity in Educational Development Internship Grant (podnetwork.org/about-us/grants-and-awards), where academics and higher education professionals can explore various roles at institutions outside of their current job. Because this kind of job shadowing occurs over a longer period of time, it is more likely that this kind of position would be paid, but unpaid internships are also possibilities.

For both short-term and long-term job shadowing opportunities, doing your research is key. You will want to make sure that you are choosing (a) the correct role to shadow, (b) people to shadow who will be reflective enough about their role for you to learn from them, (c) a good time frame (whether a day or longer) for the shadowing to occur so that you can experience a range of activities, and (d) an institution where you could see yourself working. All of this can take careful planning and coordination, and you will want to make sure that the main person you are shadowing is fully aware of your expectations for the experience.

Here are some possible areas of information to take notes on while you are completing the job shadowing experience:

- What is a typical day like in this role? What kinds of activities and events occurred?
- What did you like about what you experienced in the job shadow? What did you not like?
- Who are the people that the person you shadowed interacted with throughout the day?

Perhaps most important, you will want to ask if you can see yourself in this kind of role.

Internships

A final possibility for increasing your knowledge of an alt-ac role is to pursue an internship where you can try out the work firsthand. It's possible that your institution has positions like this available in different departments (e.g., faculty development centers frequently have "fellows" positions available for faculty who want to contribute their time to assisting their peers with teaching and learning). If you do not have positions available within your institution, consider working with a neighboring institution to create a part-time internship role. Last, you can also get creative and seek out internship roles through more nontraditional methods. For example, offer your services to a volunteer organization that needs assistance.

If you decide to pursue an internship role, here are some questions to consider as you design the experience:

- What are you hoping to learn from the internship? Are there specific skills you want to make sure that you are able to practice?
- How many hours per week or month can you devote to the internship?
- How long do you want the internship to be? Will it be short term or based on a specific project that you need to complete?
- What kind of mentoring are you hoping to experience through the internship?

Having a clear idea of what you hope to get out of an internship opportunity will help you design one that is right for you and your career stage.

Next Steps

As you review the different strategies offered in this chapter, consider which might be most appropriate for your current professional level and future career aspirations. For example, if you are in the early days of exploring an alt-ac career, the informational interviews and more covert information-gathering strategies outlined previously will probably help you more than a more intensive job shadowing experience. However, if you are a more experienced professional who is looking to make a career transition, a job shadow or internship might be just the thing you need to help you decide what next direction is right for you. Take a few minutes and write down a couple of action items that you can complete in the next week to help you learn more about alt-ac roles. These might include researching potential interview subjects or exploring some of the resources from this chapter.

As you learn more about the alt-ac career paths that are of interest to you, consider sharing what you are learning through a blog post or other public medium. Reflecting on what you learned, what questions you still have, and what you plan to do next can help you synthesize new information and connect with others who might also be interested in similar topics. Group blogging platforms, such as Medium, are excellent online communities where you can connect with others through tagging posts and commenting on other people's writing.

PART THREE

GETTING STARTED IN ALT-AC

In Part Three, we offer practical strategies related to starting down an alt-ac pathway. This part includes activities for people just beginning the process of engaging in a higher education career, such as graduate students completing their studies. For this audience, we provide resources to help graduate students talk with their advisers about choosing alt-ac careers over faculty roles. For the broader audience of anyone interested in alt-ac roles, this part also includes practical advice for preparing to hunt for jobs and engage in the interview process.

8

PREPARING FOR AN ALT-AC CAREER WHILE STILL IN GRAD SCHOOL

In this chapter, you will (a) identify alt-ac preparation activities to complete during your graduate studies and (b) identify peers who are also considering alt-ac positions to begin the process of networking.

Narrowing Your Field of Study While Expanding Your Skills

The lack of growth in tenure-track jobs described in chapter 1 is a bit scary, isn't it? If you are currently in a graduate program or are a recent graduate currently looking for a job, the pickings can be pretty slim. Graduate school is actually the perfect time to begin thinking more broadly about what kind of job might be a good fit for you. Although we are taught our whole graduate careers to become narrower in our specialties, the alt-ac mind-set is more about thinking broadly about the skills and abilities we bring to the table. In this chapter, we will be exploring some of the ways that you can start preparing yourself for the alt-ac job market while you are also wrapping up your final degree requirements.

In graduate school, all of this book's authors encountered colleagues who expanded their skill sets by taking on advising roles; working with faculty and graduate student peers through a Center for Teaching and Learning (CTL), Writing Across the Curriculum (WAC), or Writing in the Disciplines (WID) program; learning specialized research techniques through assistantships; taking on administrative positions across the university; working with community nonprofits; pursuing internships outside of their main field of study; acting in local theater projects; and working on a range of other skill-building roles. Although you may be told that you should be focusing only on your dissertation while in the final stages of your graduate program before you start the job hunt, we believe this may actually be the most flexible time you have to begin exploring other opportunities and learning new things that could help you when you go on the market.

What Skills Do You Already Have?

As you start to think about preparing yourself for an alt-ac position, one of the first important steps is to take an inventory of all the skills that you currently have that you might be able to leverage in your professional life. There are probably a lot of things that you've picked up along the way that might not have made it into that official document that is your CV (more on shaping that later). For example, are you an experienced collaborator? Do you excel at project management? Are you a strong public speaker? Here is a list of some of the more traditional academic skills that you might already have that can be leveraged for alt-ac roles:

- Teaching
- Research methods
- Assessment and evaluation methods
- Writing (include specific subgenres such as grant writing)
- Editing
- Advising

Here are just a few of the more nontraditional skills that we have picked up over time that we might add to our own lists:

- Podcasting
- Voice acting
- Blogging
- Sales and promotion
- Social media marketing
- Website design and development
- Event management
- Furniture building
- Travel hacking

Create your own list of specialized skills that you *already* bring to the table:

_____   _____

_____   _____

_____   _____

_____   _____

If you want even more skill examples, check out the list included in MLA's "Career Exploration Activity Packet" (connect.mla.hcommons.org/mla-career-exploration-activity-packet-skills-self-assessment-job-ad-analysis-and-next-steps) for additional inspiration.

What Skills Do You Need?

Now that you have identified the skills that you already have, it's time to list the kinds of skills that you know you still need to develop. These might be things that you have started to learn but still need more practice with or things that you haven't started to learn yet but know you need to start. During our own alt-ac career beginnings, these are some of the things that belonged on this list:

- Developing effective keynotes
- Understanding basic statistics
- Formulating and strengthening research design
- Writing book proposals and grants
- Drafting contracts
- Negotiating
- Managing staff effectively

All these areas were ones that we learned more about over time through formal education, reading, intentional practice, and seeking out mentors (more on this in a later chapter). Create your own list of the skills you know you *need* to develop:

_____   _____

_____   _____

_____   _____

_____   _____

What Skills Do You Want to Have?

There is a final category of skills to consider as you prepare for your alt-ac career. This category includes those things that you *want* to be able to do, even if you could probably get by without them. Even though these skill sets may not seem mandatory, you are often passionate about them for a reason, and they can enhance your professional life immensely. An excellent example of this kind of skill would be something like podcasting. Through her experiences podcasting, one of the authors, Linder, has become more skilled in public speaking, marketing, social media engagement, networking, systems thinking, sponsorship negotiation, and brand management, among other areas. All of these skill sets resulted directly from her choice to produce podcasts.

Create a list of your dream skills you know you *want* to develop:

_____	_____
_____	_____
_____	_____
_____	_____

Finding Supportive Colleagues

As you begin to explore potential alt-ac careers, it can be helpful to also start to identity people who will support you along the way. Graduate school is an excellent place to meet other alt-ac preprofessionals on whom you can rely for guidance, story-sharing, and advice, not only now but also throughout your career. Later in this book, we'll talk about other kinds of support groups that alt-acs can create or join, but while you are in graduate school, keep an eye out for those kindred spirits who are also thinking beyond the tenure track. Here are a few places to look for those peers.

In Your Department

Don't be surprised if you have alt-ac-oriented peers closer than you think. Because the academic job market has been challenging (to put it kindly) in recent years, many graduate students have started looking at employment alternatives. Consider forming a small group of peers with whom you can read about and explore alt-ac careers.

In Your Discipline

Many disciplines have started to explore how they can help graduate students look for employment beyond the tenure track. For example, the Modern Language Association (MLA) has a Committee on the Status of Graduate Students in the Profession that offers job seekers information on placement data for MLA PhDs, as well as a range of resources for the job application process.

The American Historical Association has a "Career Diversity for Historians" section of its website (www.historians.org/jobs-and-professional-development/career-diversity-for-historians). If you attend an annual conference for your field, keep an eye out for these kinds of groups where you might find other alt-ac job seekers.

Online Communities

Social media platforms are excellent places to find like-minded alt-ac-oriented peers. Start by searching the #altac hashtag to find conversations that might interest you. You can also "follow" or "friend" people in alt-ac jobs that you find interesting. More formal online communities like Beyond the Professoriate (community.beyondprof.com) host interviews, webinars, and online conferences for non-tenure-track academics and higher education professionals who have chosen alt-ac career pathways.

Next Steps

If you think an alt-ac career might be for you, a good place to start is to research all the different kinds of jobs in your field and discipline. As you begin to talk about your alt-ac career plans with others (more on this later in this book), the more you know about the range of possibilities in front of you, the better. In addition to the resources mentioned in Part Two of this book, here are some places to start your research:

- Your department or the graduate departments of other schools that train people in your field or discipline may have alumni job placement data that you can explore; sometimes this information is even included on a department website as a selling point for the program.
- If your field or discipline has an electronic mailing list, review the archives to see the job advertisements that have been posted there.
- If your field or discipline has a national organization, check to see if its website has a job board or if it collects job placement data for the organization's members. Good examples can be found on the MLA website mentioned previously (www.mla.org), as well as on the websites for the American Geophysical Union (sites.agu.org), the American Anthropological Association (www.americananthro .org), and the American Historical Association (www.historians .org).

- Job postings in industry publications such as *The Chronicle of Higher Education* or *Inside Higher Ed* are another great place to explore the range of job opportunities available within higher education.

The following chapters will offer you additional advice about talking through the alt-ac career trajectory with your adviser and preparing to go on the alt-ac job market.

9

GETTING YOUR PARTNER
OR FAMILY ON BOARD
WITH THE DECISION
TO GO ALT-AC

In this chapter, you will (a) prepare to discuss your alt-ac decisions with various people in your life, (b) develop a goal statement for what you want to achieve via alt-ac positions, and (c) create an outline of how your graduate or doctoral work has prepared you for an alt-ac role.

Addressing Great Expectations

A growing number of doctoral or terminal degree seekers already have alt-ac careers in mind—as the ultimate goal or a potential fallback position. On one hand, you may have been working in an alt-ac position when you started a graduate program to further your existing career. On the other hand, many graduate students enter and/or leave their degree programs with the dream of becoming a full-time, tenure-track faculty member. However you see your degree and its relationship to your career, chances are good that others may see you differently. From their vantage point, they may know only that you worked for years toward a very specific academic goal. In some cases, the graduate degrees, the postdoctoral work, and the academic world in general may be mysteries to those who support you. In other cases, your loved ones may have built up their own expectations about what you should do after you graduate.

As you investigate alt-ac positions and careers, you may have to consider how your career decisions affect those closest to you, how their reactions affect you, or both. Maybe you've overheard your mother on the phone saying something like "I'm so proud of my daughter. She's going to be a professor!" Perhaps your partner or spouse is already on the tenure track, coaching and encouraging you to reach the same goal. On the flip side, your partner may not understand your goals or academia in general and may want you to start working rather than continuing to pursue academic positions.

Less specifically, your children may have said they wished you did not have to take any more night and weekend classes or study so much even when you are at home. Or your partner or spouse has supported you as you complete your graduate studies and write your dissertation—emotionally, financially, or otherwise, giving you time (and space) to write, taking care of the kids, doing most of the cooking, you name it. It may just be a matter of not wanting to let down or disappoint those who have cheered you on as you pursued tenure-track goals. Faced with spoken and unspoken expectations, it can be difficult to tell those in your innermost circle of family and friends that your goals have changed.

Developing a Goal Statement

As you prepare for these conversations, you can use a goal statement to show others how pursuing a temporary alt-ac position or a more permanent alt-ac career allows you to achieve some or all of the goals you set for yourself as a tenure-track faculty member. In some cases, you may even exceed them! So, let's start there. What are or were some of the motivations or drivers behind wanting a tenure-track faculty position? Motivations might include preparing students to enter your field in real-world settings or inspiring them to achieve their own dreams, working with like-minded colleagues in an academic setting, or making contributions to your discipline through research or publications. You may have included some of those drivers in a research statement and/or teaching philosophy as you prepared for the tenure-track application process. Make a note of those underlying motivations here:

_____

_____

_____

When you start crafting a goal statement, consider how those same motivations or drivers work in an alt-ac context. If your research is what gets you up in the morning, then find non-tenure-track pathways to stay engaged in research that fits your goals. If teaching feeds your soul, then consider applying for a part-time contingent or adjunct faculty position to augment other work. If your motivations are tied to your discipline, then mapping them to an alt-ac context may be easier said than done. Goal statements like "research opportunities in biomedical sciences" or "adjunct teaching positions in classical studies" focus on specific positions rather than the underlying motivations. Construct a goal statement that gets at the heart of what drives you and provide you with the greatest flexibility in reaching it.

Think back to the personal statement you may have needed to submit for your graduate program. You might have identified interests and past experiences that influenced your career decisions and goals. These same ideas can help you to think about how to use your doctoral work to support an alt-ac career. Look at your old personal statements and reflect on what has changed. What remains true? How well does this previous statement characterize your new career goals, whether they involve an alt-ac profession or alt-ac positions until you join the tenure track? If you did not have to submit a personal statement and have not done this exercise before, think in terms of goals over roles.

When Andrea Colangelo decided to earn an EdD degree, she did so for personal growth. She felt that she had been on a narrow path teaching English, and the degree program expanded her view of the humanistic elements of education. Seeing the field through other people's lenses and stories—those of her instructors and her peers—was a vital part of the experience. At the same time, she did not have concrete career goals in mind as she sought her degree. A few years after earning her EdD, she came to realize that she had landed on the alt-ac path coming on the heels of changes in the job market. There were fewer new tenure-track jobs available, and existing positions were not opening up, in part because tenured faculty were not retiring as soon as they had previously.

Colangelo wants to combine her love of the academic environment with other needs. She wants to research, write, teach, and present, and she feels she can perform all of these through a job outside the tenure track. She wants to guide students to success, and she finds it rewarding and meaningful to do this as an academic coach. In her counseling role, she feels she is able to give more time to each student than if she had become a full-time faculty member. With 45-minute appointments instead of 10-minute office hour visits, she can provide encouragement and motivation along with the practical academic support.

Her current three- to five-year goal involves working toward being an assistant director of a writing or learning center. She would prefer to work at the university level so she can work with graduate students—especially doctoral students. Colangelo just accepted a position in an academic skills center at a community college near her home. (It was the first time in five years she has been able to drive to the interview rather than fly to another city.) She wants to learn the culture of the organization and get to know the diverse needs of community college students before trying to move into an assistant director position. She will focus on helping those students build foundational skills—a new challenge after working primarily with graduate students in her previous positions.

However, Colangelo has not lost sight of her research goals. During the interview with her new boss, she asked about the possibility of conducting research at the center, such as studying the effectiveness of the support they provide. To stay on track with all of her goals, Colangelo conducts self-check-ins daily—a habit she learned as a child by watching her parents do the same as teachers. She likes to grow through conferences; professional development training; and, most of all, observing others.

Outlining Applicable Experience

Creating a current goal statement is a good exercise, regardless of where you are on your career journey. Having that statement will also help clarify your thinking and frame conversations with family and friends. It is likely that your underlying goals have not changed as much as the roles you may pursue to achieve them. Furthermore, you can highlight the value of earning your degree by identifying new knowledge, skills, attitudes, and experiences that have prepared or will prepare you to work toward those professional goals, regardless of what job you take.

One way to approach this activity is to create a "job description" of your graduate work. You might list skills related to research, such as identifying gaps in the research, developing study protocols or data collection instruments, conducting experiments with specialized equipment, or analyzing results. Skills related to writing might include translating quantitative data to language that has meaning for people unfamiliar with the discipline, supporting and defending arguments through analysis of related or comparable studies, and editing and formatting academic documents for publication. You might have additional skills related to advising, evaluation, teaching, administration, or management.

Here are some questions that might help get the ball rolling. Are there discipline-specific knowledge and/or approaches to problem-solving that you have used or mastered? Did you have to follow specific standards or regulations? Did you work on or manage a team? Did you engage with the public in some way? Did you gain teaching experience? Did you have extraordinary experiences during your graduate work that prepared you for similar work as a professional? Take a minute to document aspects of your graduate work that support you in reaching your professional goals.

_____

_____

_____

_____

_____

_____

Next Steps

Now that you have reviewed the ideas in this chapter and engaged in some preliminary thinking, it's time to start your own goal statement. If you want more direction, you can use personal statement prompts like these generic questions by Doran and Brizee (2012):

- "When did you become interested in this field and what have you learned about it (and about yourself) that has further stimulated your interest and reinforced your conviction that you are well suited to this field? What insights have you gained?"
- "What personal characteristics (for example, integrity, compassion, and/or persistence) do you possess that would improve your prospects for success in the field or profession? Is there a way to demonstrate or document that you have these characteristics?"

Prompts specific to transferring skills and knowledge to an alt-ac position might include the following:

- How have your interests in this field changed over time? How have they remained constant or been reinforced by your graduate work?
- Now that you have gained expertise in a specific area, how do you imagine using it professionally? In what ways do you envision improving an existing process or product?
- Describe professional applications of your past and present research. Is there still research to perform in a specific area?

Once you have answered a few of these prompts or your own, synthesize your answers into a brief statement. Share it with your family to see how it resonates. They may have feedback or questions that will help you create a strong, final version.

Next, review your bullet list of the knowledge, skills, attitudes, and experiences that you gained as a graduate student. Start organizing them into categories. If you need help doing this, try putting each item on a separate sticky note and organizing them on a table or a wall. Once you have grouped them in different ways, write short paragraphs outlining how those experiences have prepared you to reach the goal(s) you made for yourself. Make calendar entries to remind you to revisit both the goal and the outline over time, as you will continue to grow in whatever alt-ac position you take.

Last, prepare mentally for conversations with people close to you. Consider your decision from the perspectives of the people you need or decide to tell, especially if the idea of your pursuing an alt-ac career will be new to them. They may ask tough questions about different aspects of going alt-ac that you may not have considered, such as the following:

- Emotional: "Do you feel like you're giving up?"
- Logistical: "Will we have to move for you to pursue an alt-ac career?"
- Financial: "Will alt-ac positions pay enough for us to cover our monthly rent, mortgage, expenses, and so on?"
- Social: "What do you want me to tell people?"

General career guidance articles (e.g., Boogaard, n.d.; Stanley, n.d.) provide some good ideas about having conversations with family and friends to get them on board:

- Listening to each person to understand different viewpoints and concerns can help you avoid emotional reactions.
- Involving your loved ones (beyond just telling them) not only helps get their buy-in but also encourages them to support and help you.

Natasha Stanley (n.d.) closes with some valuable advice: "Speak from the heart" because "ultimately, your friends and family want you to be happy."

COMMUNICATING ABOUT ALT-AC CAREERS WITH GRADUATE ADVISERS

In this chapter, you will (a) examine the depth of your relationship with your adviser and your adviser's thoughts about academic and alt-ac careers and (b) prepare for discussions with your adviser about your future after graduating.

Kathryn E. Linder's Story: Pursuing an Alt-Ac Faculty Development Role

In graduate school, when Linder shared her plans to go on the job market to pursue an alt-ac job in faculty development, her adviser was not thrilled. Because her degree was in a smaller, interdisciplinary field that was still relatively young (women's and gender studies), it seemed important to her adviser to place graduates in tenure-track roles to boost the reputation of the department.

However, when Linder went on the job market, the tenure-track jobs available in her field were in highly specialized areas that were unrelated to her dissertation and interests. While Linder's adviser certainly had her best interests at heart, she had spent most of her career at the same institution in the same tenure-track job and had risen to the rank of full professor. For many senior faculty member advisers, newer alt-ac possibilities for graduate students are unfamiliar and can appear, at least on the surface, as less stable.

Stories of graduate students having to defend their choice to pursue an alt-ac career trajectory are becoming more common as more graduate students are considering alt-ac roles. While your adviser can be one of the most important assets that you have on the job market, ironically, they may really only be prepared to help you get on the tenure track. Your adviser knows your work more intimately than anyone else and is in the position of writing a strong letter of recommendation to your potential future employer, but you may need something different if you plan to pursue an alt-ac role. In this chapter, we will provide you with some tools and strategies to begin this conversation with your adviser, including a set of questions and prompts that you can use to get the discussion rolling.

Preparing to Break the News

Breaking the news to your adviser that you are not planning to go on the job market for a tenure-track role can be a challenging conversation to have. We have heard stories of graduate students who have lost the support of their adviser entirely or advisers who now considered their graduate student a waste of time. These stories are incredibly unfortunate and—we hope—few and far between. As you prepare for this conversation with your adviser, keep in mind these steps you can take to get ready.

Talk to Previous Advisees

Sometimes it can be easy to forget that we might not be the only ones going through this process. It is possible that there are alums or current students in your department who have already broken the ice with your adviser regarding alt-ac careers. You may already know about some of these people, or you can start quietly asking around to see if you can find others who can share their experience and offer advice because they have been there, done that.

Practice, Practice, Practice

Talking with your adviser can be an intimidating experience, and this is a pretty important conversation to have, so don't underestimate the importance of practicing. Think through the main points that are the most important to convey and say the words out loud a few times so that the first time you are hearing them is not in your adviser's office. Picturing yourself in the space where the conversation will take place may also help calm your nerves.

Anticipate Questions

Of course, your adviser will have questions! Given what you know about your adviser, think ahead of time about possible questions and how you might want to answer them. Here are some possible questions to prepare for:

- How long have you been thinking about this?
- Are you sure you don't want to pursue the tenure track? You are such a good researcher [teacher, scholar, and so on]!
- Why are you pursuing a PhD if you do not want to become a professor?
- What does your spouse [partner, parents, family, and so on] think about this?
- How do you know you'll be able to find an alt-ac job?
- Isn't the alt-ac job market even more unstable because there's no tenure?

And, if you are lucky, you'll get asked this:

- How can I help?

Breaking the News

When talking with your adviser about alt-ac roles for the first time, you may want to assume they know very little about the alt-ac career trajectory. Indeed, alt-ac roles are probably quite different from your adviser's own career experience. One possibility is to hand your adviser a copy of this book—we did write it, in part, to make these kinds of conversations easier—but here are some other conversation starters that might be useful:

- What are your general impressions of the job market in our field or discipline?
- Have you ever considered a job outside the tenure track? Why or why not?
- Are you familiar with the term *alt-ac*?
- Do you have any previous advisees who have pursued careers outside of the traditional tenure-track role?
- When you think about my skills and abilities, what stands out to you as my particular strengths that I can leverage on the job market?

These questions will help you enter into the beginning stages of a conversation with your adviser about what's next for you and your career. Many advisers want what is best for their advisees. Your adviser is probably no different.

Dealing With a Resistant Adviser

So that conversation didn't go so well, huh? Fortunately, we are "prepare for the best, plan for the worst" sorts of authors. If your adviser is not as excited as you are about your future as an alt-ac professional, the most important thing to know is *that's okay*. Alt-ac positions are somewhat disruptive to the traditions of the academy, and the academic world is changing—probably faster than many faculty members would like. It may take a little while for your adviser to catch up to the ideas that you have probably been thinking about for several weeks, if not months or years. If your initial conversation does not go the way you are hoping, here are some strategies to consider.

Wait Them Out

It is entirely possible that your adviser just needs some time to process what you have said. It can be difficult news when a potential protégé decides to move in a different direction than was originally planned. After your initial conversation, give your adviser some time to think and reflect before you circle back.

Offer Data

In addition to sharing this book, you might want to share any disciplinary-specific data you have collected about job placement prospects in your field. As we mentioned in the previous chapter, many national disciplinary organizations are tracking job placement for PhDs and are aware of the growing alt-ac choices that many are making.

Get Personal

It might not be clear to your adviser that this is a choice you are making because you *want* to, not a choice you are making because you *have* to. Some advisers see the choice of an alt-ac career as kind of giving up, and this is absolutely incorrect. Share how you came to this decision over much time and reflection to see if you can sway your adviser a bit. Show your adviser your multiyear career map (see chapter 6) and/or an outline of how you plan to use the skills you have gained as a graduate student in an alt-ac context (see chapter 16).

Ask for What You Need

Even if your adviser is less than enthusiastic about your career choices, they might still need to play an important role in your job search as a reference. If this is the case, give your adviser specific guidance about what you need and when, so that your adviser can better assist you. Remember that your adviser may be used to writing the typical tenure-track reference letter, which can be significantly different from what you might need for an alt-ac application.

Sever Ties

In some more drastic cases, we are aware of graduate students who have transitioned to another adviser if their current adviser was completely unsupportive of their alt-ac plans. Although this is certainly a worst-case scenario and can be quite disruptive to your graduate career time line, it is an option. If you think this is the only option for you to pursue, talk with trusted colleagues or your department chair about potentially switching to another adviser. Also, keep in mind that shifting this relationship can add significant time to completing the degree, especially for graduate students in the sciences who may need to switch labs along with advisers.

Next Steps

Remember Linder's story from the beginning of the chapter? We are pleased to share that it had a happy ending. If you fast-forward a year from Linder's initial conversation with her adviser, you would find that Linder was one of the only graduates in her cohort to immediately land a job within higher education. She even started the job before defending her dissertation. In the years to follow, other graduate students from the department would pursue apprenticeships in faculty development—some at the encouragement of their advisers—and follow in Linder's footsteps to pursue alt-ac jobs. Linder's adviser continues to be one of her biggest supporters and was included in the dedication of her third book.

A favorite resource of ours for difficult conversations is from Stone, Patton, and Heen (2010). In *Difficult Conversations: How to Discuss What Matters Most*, the authors offered specific strategies to help you prepare for and survive conversations that you know will be challenging. A few of their quick tips are to get curious about the other person's story, to separate out intent from impact, and to speak with clarity and power. Although we hope the very best for all of your discussions about alt-ac, this resource is a helpful one as you prepare to get your adviser on board.

II

JOB HUNTING

In this chapter, you will identify pathways and online resources to find alt-ac job opportunities.

Starting the Job Hunt

Once you have had a chance to explore a range of alt-ac job possibilities, it's time to get real with the job hunt. One of the most important ways that you can get started with your job search is to have a sense of what you are looking for. Here are some questions to help you find the right alt-ac job for you:

- Are you looking for a position within higher education, in an industry outside of higher education, or both? (Refer back to chapters 3 and 4 to get ideas for positions on a campus or "beyond the campus.")
- Do you have a sense of the position titles you might be eligible for?
- Do you know anyone who has recently been hired into an alt-ac job? If yes, how did that person find the position opening?
- Is your alt-ac search public, or are you engaging in a more covert job hunt?

Each of these questions will help as you get started with finding open positions that you might want to apply to.

Before you start searching, it can also be useful to have your list of musts and must-nots for your ideal alt-ac job. For example:

- Do you have any geographical limitations for your new job?
- Do you have a minimum salary requirement for your new job?
- Are you looking for full-time work only, or are you open to part-time positions?
- Is there a specific level of job title that is a minimum requirement for you?

- Is there a specific job that will provide necessary or valuable experience for you to reach your ultimate professional goal(s)?

Ask yourself these questions as a way to sketch out some basic parameters for yourself regarding the open positions that you identify as possibilities in the job search process.

Finding Alt-Ac Jobs

Fortunately, there are several different ways to learn about alt-ac jobs. Some of these methods are through online tools and services, while others are based on in-person networking.

Online Job Hunt Resources

The following online resource categories fall into two categories: searching for job opportunities on your own and searching through other people.

Disciplinary Job Boards

Many discipline-specific national and regional organizations post jobs to their websites. This may be a member benefit or in a publicly accessible area.

Industry Job Boards

Industry publications for higher education such as *The Chronicle of Higher Education* and *Inside Higher Ed* have searchable job boards where many institutions post their open positions. There are also several other websites devoted to helping higher education professionals find open positions such as HigherEdJobs (www.higheredjobs.com) and the HERC (www.hercjobs .org). If you are interested in an industry outside of higher education, check to see if there is a publication or organization where jobs are commonly posted. Turn back to chapter 4 to see examples of job boards run by government agencies, research institutes and labs, professional associations, and cultural organizations.

Human Resources Websites

If you have a specific target for where you know you want to work or even a specific region of the country, you can always go directly to the source and look at the human resources websites to see what job openings they have. Not all universities and companies use the larger curated job posting sites, so this can be a strategy to find jobs that might otherwise fly under your radar.

Social Networking Platforms

Online platforms such as LinkedIn and ResearchGate and social media sites such as Twitter are all places where openings are posted and shared. Depending on the strength of your profile, sites like LinkedIn may also e-mail or post suggestions of jobs or positions that might be a good fit for you.

Electronic Mailing Lists and Discussion Groups

If your career area of interest has an electronic mailing list, it is possible that job openings are being posted and advertised there. Pay attention to the kinds of positions that are posted or look in the electronic mailing list archives to see trends and patterns in the industry that you are interested in. Check to see if your graduate school has a discussion group where alumni post new job opportunities.

In-Person Job Hunt Resources

The following activities and resources all involve working with others to find and pursue job opportunities.

Conference Job Fairs

If you attend a conference related to your discipline or career area of interest, check to see if there is a job fair or job postings available on-site. Some conferences even offer private spaces to conduct interviews at the conference itself.

Colleagues

Never underestimate the power of networking. Your colleagues can be an excellent source of information when you are job searching if they know the kind of position that you are looking for. Before you go to a conference, for example, send a message to any electronic mailing lists or discussion groups to identify if anyone you know virtually will be attending. Set up networking meetings for coffee, breakfast, lunch, dinner, drinks, or even a hallway chat during breaks between sessions to connect and network with colleagues throughout the event. Not attending conferences? You can also do this kind of networking via e-mail or social media. Keep in mind that depending on your level of experience, colleagues can also be a great resource for recommending you for jobs that involve search firms.

Search Firms

Speaking of search firms, if you are a more experienced alt-ac professional, you may be eligible for positions that involve recruitment from search firms. These positions are often higher level roles within a university or company. Search firms are always looking for strong candidates, and as you build your professional reputation, it will become more likely that you will be "head-hunted" or cold-called by a search firm about an open position that might be of interest to you.

Past Successes

As you think about how you plan to go about finding your ideal alt-ac position, reflect on how you found your last job. Did you answer an online ad, hear about it from a friend, or see a flyer posted somewhere? Thinking about what has worked for you in the past might give you some ideas for what could work in your current job hunt.

Next Steps

Ready to get started? Search away! Begin exploring the resources in this chapter to see if you can identify three to five potential alt-ac jobs that might be a good fit for your skills, abilities, and career aspirations. Once you have those positions identified, continue reading to learn more about preparing your job application materials and preparing yourself for all the different kinds of interviews that you might encounter throughout the job search process. Can't get enough resources on the job hunt? Check out Bolles (2018) for one of the most canonical resources on finding a job and changing careers. *What Color Is Your Parachute?* has been the go-to guide for job seekers for years and is considered to be one of the world's most popular career guides. The self-inventories are an excellent resource for those just starting a new job hunt, and the book also includes tips and strategies for interviewing, salary negotiation, and more.

12

PREPARING ALT-AC
JOB MATERIALS

In this chapter, you will review the differences and similarities between alt-ac job materials and faculty job materials.

Common Alt-Ac Position Application Materials

So you have decided to apply for that alt-ac job. Hooray! Your next questions might be about what you can expect regarding job materials required for an application. While there are certainly some similarities between alt-ac job materials and the materials you would prepare for a traditional faculty application, there are some key differences as well. In the following sections, we break down the key components of alt-ac job application materials: the CV and résumé, cover letters, statements of various kinds, and references and reference letters (the next chapter covers the interview stage, so stay tuned for that). This chapter is also a great resource to share with an adviser or other people who are supporting you in seeking an alt-ac role, especially if they are unfamiliar with alt-ac career models.

CV and Résumé

Depending on your career stage and previous work experience, you may have already created both a CV and a résumé. Both of these documents are meant to offer a road map of your professional accomplishments over time. A résumé is the simpler of the two documents and is often only one to two pages in length. This document includes information about your educational history, your work experience, and your contact information. Sometimes résumés also include information about specific skill sets that you have related to the position you are applying for.

In comparison, a CV is a much more comprehensive document that not only details all of the components included in a résumé but also offers information about your publications, presentations, grants and awards, and other aspects of your professional life that have accumulated over time to tell the story of your career. The job posting will outline whether a CV or résumé is required for a specific job application, but keep in mind that each of these documents should be tailored to the job to which you are applying.

If you are creating one of these documents for the first time, or if you are converting a CV to a résumé, we recommend first seeking out examples. There are several places to find examples of these documents, including HigherEdJobs (www.higheredjobs.com/popup/ResumeSample1.cfm) and many institutional career centers, such as the resources from the University of Wisconsin–Madison (merit-www.education.wisc.edu/epcs/students-alumni/prepare-connect/personal-marketing-tools). For a more detailed exploration of CVs and résumés, we recommend Linder (2018), which includes a chapter on designing these documents effectively for a range of purposes, including going on the job market.

Cover Letters

While the standard faculty position cover letter might include a paragraph each for your teaching, research, and service experience, an alt-ac position cover letter might look significantly different. For example, in a typical alt-ac cover letter, you probably should not talk about your dissertation (unless your research is directly applicable to the job you are applying for). Although this may seem like sacrilege, especially because your dissertation has been such a large part of your life for quite some time, the truth is that it may just not be relevant to your alt-ac career aspirations. Cover letters typically range from one to two pages, although they can be longer for higher level administrative positions. As you are drafting a cover letter for your alt-ac applications, keep the following principles in mind.

It's as Much About Them as It Is About You

Although we often think about cover letters as being all about us and the kinds of skills and experiences we bring to a particular job, it is important to start the cover letter writing process by thinking first about what your potential future employer will be looking for. An in-depth review of the job description can offer key words and phrases that should be included in the cover letter to show how perfect you are for the role.

Cover Letters Serve Only One Purpose

Cover letters have a single goal: to get you to the next stage of the interview process. Therefore, you are just trying to make it very difficult for the search committee to say that you are not a qualified candidate. In some institutions, search committees are applying a rubric of criteria (taken directly from the job description) to your initial application materials. Make sure that you overtly point to all the ways that you are qualified for the position so that you get moved to the next stage.

It's Okay to Say You Want the Job

All three authors of this book have read too many cover letters where we were not even sure that the candidates actually wanted the jobs. Being *too* formal in a cover letter can mean that you never actually say why you were initially drawn to the job or that you are excited for the opportunity to apply. Sharing these sentiments is completely appropriate and may differentiate you from more stoic cover letter writers.

You Are Writing to Potential Future Colleagues

It is a little strange to think that the people reading your letter could, in a matter of weeks or months, be the people you are chatting with over the office coffee machine. However, keeping this in mind can help you strike the right tone of professionalism and personality in your cover letter. If your goal is to stand out enough to get to the next stage of interviewing, then inserting some of your personality into the cover letter can help you get there. Consider sharing about a favorite past project that overlaps with the job requirements or an exciting new skill area you are developing. Be careful about using humor, because it can be interpreted—and misinterpreted—in a range of ways by different people, but definitely be yourself.

Statements of Various Kinds

It is not uncommon for alt-ac position descriptions to include a request for you to write a statement about your experience with a particular area. Sometimes these are also called descriptions of your philosophy on a topic or issue. Here are some potential examples:

- Your statement or philosophy of leadership
- Your statement or philosophy regarding diversity and inclusion

- Your statement or philosophy related to a specific component of the job description (e.g., a faculty development position might have you write about how you consult with faculty clients)

These statements can be quite challenging to write because they are a unique subgenre of the application materials portfolio. They are usually relatively short—often one to two pages—and require you to distill complex topics down to some main points. If you are asked to write such a statement, consider the following advice to get you started.

Read the Prompt Carefully
If you are asked to write some kind of statement or philosophy, it is common to be given a prompt of at least one to two sentences, sometimes more, to get you started. Read the prompt several times to make sure that you are responding directly to what is being asked of you.

Read the Prompt in Context
Search committees ask for these statements for a reason. Consider the statement within the context of the job itself, with the other application materials (e.g., you do not want to be too repetitive with your cover letter), and with the institution as a whole. For example, if you are asked to write a statement on diversity and inclusion, do a little research to see if the institution has recently engaged in any processes clarifying its own stance on the same topic. You might find that it has recently updated its mission, hired a chief diversity officer, or provided other evidence of its commitment to diversity and inclusion that should be referenced in your statement.

Be Reflective
These statements are meant to be a true representation about what you believe about a certain topic or issue. To that end, it can be useful to do some reflective writing or chatting with a colleague or two about your thoughts before you begin to write the statement.

Take Your Time
It is not uncommon for these kinds of statements to take multiple drafts before you feel comfortable with submitting them. Try to give yourself at least a few days to work on the draft of your statement.

Get Specific

Using examples from your past experience to offer the reader a clear window into your thoughts on the topic or issue at hand can be very useful. Rather than making abstract statements, get as concrete as you can with specific examples.

Choose Three Main Points

Remember that five-paragraph essay from your early writing days? This is the perfect assignment to use that model. Pick the three main things (four if you must) that you want to discuss and offer a paragraph (or two) for each one. This structure will help you stay on point and organized.

Get Personal

We don't think you should share your life story, but it is important to personalize your statement so that it does not sound like every other statement the search committee will read. This means staying away from platitudes and offering the kinds of specific examples of your experience that we recommended earlier.

References and Reference Letters

Job searches are never conducted completely on your own. In addition to the support of your friends and family, you also have your references as a support structure throughout the process. In this section, we offer some key things to keep in mind as you are identifying who will best serve as a reference and as a reference letter writer during your alt-ac job search.

References

We have yet to see an academic job application process that does not require the inclusion of references. These references are often people who can be called in the later stages of the search process to speak to your skills and character. As you are thinking of whom you want to ask to serve as a reference, you will want to consider who can best speak to your skills and abilities with specific examples. It is helpful to have references who have known you professionally for quite some time and who have seen you perform well in a variety of situations.

References can be a bit touchy, especially if you are hunting for a new job while in another position. Many search committees offer the courtesy of asking your permission to contact your references before they actually do (this is sometimes even assured in the references section of the application), but this is not always the case. We recommend that you ask the permission of your references before you include them in your job application materials so that they are not caught off guard if the search committee contacts them prior to asking for your permission. You will also want to provide your references with the job description and job materials that you submitted with your application so that they have some context about the position before they receive a reference call. If there are specific things you are hoping that your references can emphasize, tell them in advance so that they have time to reflect and prepare.

One caveat to this advice is your current supervisor if you are conducting your job search on the sly. Although you will not want your supervisor contacted out of the blue, you might also not want to alert your supervisor to your job search too early. In this case, we recommend including your supervisor in your references list but not sharing about your job search until you have reached a more advanced stage of the search process (i.e., an invitation for an interview).

It is also important when approaching your references to offer them an easy way to decline. You want to ensure that you have the strongest references possible, so if they are hesitant in any way, it's better that they not serve in this capacity for you. With your request, just include a short statement such as "If for any reason this isn't a good time for you to do this, please don't hesitate to let me know." This allows your potential reference to politely decline without needing to state why.

Reference Letters

While some alt-ac jobs will just require references alone, other alt-ac jobs may require letters of reference. In these cases, rather than the standard letter from your adviser discussing how great of a researcher or teacher you are, you will most likely be seeking out a range of other references who can provide evidence of how skilled you are in relation to the specific job you are applying for. When you are choosing the people who will write your letters, it can be useful to think of the colleagues you have worked with who can speak to the following:

- Your value and/or abilities as an employee (i.e., a previous supervisor)
- Your ability to collaborate and work with others
- Your ability to solve problems
- Your ability to manage complex projects or tasks
- Your ability to supervise others
- Your ability to manage a budget

- Your specific experience with important skills or elements of the job description for the position to which you are applying

As you reach out to your letter writers, you will want to provide them with the job description for the position you are applying for, a copy of your updated CV or résumé, and a short description of what you hope they can speak to regarding your skills or experience. This ensures that you will have some diversity across your letters of reference and that your letter writers will not inadvertently all talk about the same things.

Also, it is now becoming a more common practice for those requesting the letter to actually draft it on behalf of the letter writer and then ask them to review, modify, and sign it. Some letter writers will just request bullet points of important information for them to include. This can be especially useful if you are reaching out to an adviser or previous supervisor who is not up-to-date with your current work or projects.

We also recommend sending your letter writers a quick reminder before the deadline. One way to do this is by politely checking in about their progress and asking whether they have any additional questions for you. This is also another time where you can give them an "out" to ensure that your letters are as strong as possible.

Next Steps

As you begin to prepare materials for your alt-ac job search, we recommend reviewing what you already have. Gather the current versions of your CV and/or résumé and update them, review older copies of cover letters you created in the past to see if anything might be useful for future versions, and pull out any statements or philosophy documents you created. If you do not have current versions of these documents, that's okay—you can just get started with drafting the different documents as you need them.

If you are planning to apply to multiple different alt-ac positions, then create some templated versions of your cover letter. Because this is the document that often needs the most tweaking for each application package you will be creating, it can be the most time-consuming to draft. We recommend writing targeted paragraphs for specific areas that you might want to highlight regarding your professional skills and abilities. For example, you might have a paragraph about your collaboration experience, your project management skills, or your leadership abilities. Although not all of these paragraphs will be used for every cover letter, they will give you a place to start from for each new draft you create.

If you have work products that you feel represent your abilities more fully than a CV or résumé alone, then consider creating an electronic portfolio, or ePortfolio, or a professional website. Include items such as final versions of reports that you are allowed to share, conference presentation slides or recordings, copies of publications, and links to project websites that are current. For each item, write a brief reflection that highlights what potential employers should know about you and your abilities. Last but not least, remember to share links to your ePortfolio or professional website from your CV and/or résumé. See chapter 25 for more ideas about building and sharing your portfolio.

13

INTERVIEWING

In this chapter, you will review the differences and similarities between alt-ac job interviews and faculty job interviews.

Preparing for Interviews

All alt-ac job searches will involve an interview stage and sometimes a series of interviews. If you have completed interviews in the past for faculty positions, or if you have attended professional development workshops or actual faculty interviews, you may be familiar with the components included: discussions of your dissertation or research plans; job talks with short lectures on topics related to your research; teaching demonstrations; and meetings with department chairs, deans, or other campus leadership. Alt-ac job interviews usually involve none of these elements. Moreover, you may be interviewing for an alt-ac job that is not on a college or university campus.

The kinds of activities included in alt-ac job interviews can be as wide-ranging as the alt-ac jobs themselves. In this chapter, we outline some of the key components to consider in phone and video conference interviews, as well as in on-site interviews.

Phone Interviews

The phone interview stage of the alt-ac job search, just like the initial application materials, serves a primary purpose: to get you to the next stage of the process, or the on-site interview. If the search committee asks you to complete a phone interview, that means they are interested in you as a candidate for the position. The phone interview is often a stage where the search committee is trying to narrow down the pool for the on-site interviews. If you've made it this far, you are already part of an elite section of candidates. There are several ways that you can prepare for a phone interview.

Do Your Research

We authors have all been in the position of interviewing candidates who clearly had not done any research about the position they were interviewing for or the organization itself. At the very least, check out the main website for the institution, company, or unit offering the job for which you are applying. Review the organization's mission statement, recent accomplishments, new initiatives, and any kind of strategic planning documents that you can find online. While you do not need to know everything (and it's just not possible!), having this basic information at the ready before your phone interview is always a good thing.

Know Who Will Be on the Call

Most initial phone interviews are with the search committee members, and this group can represent a range of different positions from around the university or company. It is possible that a human resources representative will also be present on the call. If you are not provided with the information of who will be on the call with you beforehand, feel free to ask the person who reached out to you to schedule the call. It is a common courtesy for them to tell you whom you can expect to speak with.

Have Some Good Questions Prepared

At the end of almost any phone interview, you will be asked what questions you have about the position. Preparing some good questions in advance will ensure that you do not freeze up at this stage of the interview. The research you conducted to prepare for the phone interview is the best way to develop some questions specific to the position, but here are some other questions that might be a good starting point:

- Who are the key stakeholders that this position collaborates with the most?
- What are the key problems and challenges you want the person hired for this position to tackle right away?
- What are the most important skills or abilities that you think the person hired for this position needs to have?

Be in a Quiet Space

Wherever you are completing the phone interview, try to ensure that you will not be interrupted by roommates, partners, colleagues, children, pets, construction noise, or any other distraction that can take away from the focus of you as a candidate.

Smile

Smiling while speaking changes the tone of your voice and the energy that you are sharing in a conversation occurring over the phone. Smiling is also a small trick that can help settle your nerves if you are anxious during the interview.

Breathe

Take a breath before you answer each question. This will allow you to compose your thoughts and will prevent you from interrupting the interviewer. Along with smiling, you can calm yourself with deep breaths into your abdomen—these will activate your vagus nerve and trigger a relaxation response.

Skype or Video Conference Interviews

Because of advances in technology, more and more search committees are choosing video conferencing for this stage of the interview process. For Skype or other video interviews, many of the same elements of the phone interview discussed previously still apply. Here are some additional things to consider.

Test Your Technology

No matter how experienced you are with Skype and other video platforms, testing your audio and video technology with a friend or colleague at least half an hour before your interview is always recommended. For example, you may need to download a browser plug-in or update to the latest version of the software. Also, make sure to use a headset or earbuds with a microphone to avoid creating an echo effect. You never want technology snafus to distract from your candidacy for a position, so troubleshoot any issues before the big event.

Find a Well-Lit Space

You want to make sure that the people you are talking to can see you, which means making sure that you are not backlit (i.e., with an unshaded window behind you). Having a strong overhead light can also ensure that you are not in shadow.

Review Your Surroundings

While we do not necessarily recommend going so far as to stage the space you will be in for your video interview, we do think it can be useful to review the space behind you to make sure that you remove things like office trash cans, family photos on the wall (which may share more personal details than you prefer at this stage), or other items that you do not want the search committee to see. As you would for a phone interview, make sure you join the video conference call from a space where you will not be interrupted by ringing office phones or mobile phones or people or pets walking by or entering the room.

Dress Professionally

This should go without saying, but because your interviewers can see you, you will definitely want to make sure that you are professionally attired for this conversation.

On-Site Interviews

Whew! You made it to the on-site interview stage. You are now in the most elite group of the interview candidates. No pressure. The on-site interview stage is the final set of interviews you will complete before your potential employer decides whether to extend you a job offer. Therefore, on-site interviews are often about that nebulous criterion called "fit." On-site interviewers are usually looking at several aspects when they interact with you in real life. One aspect is how you perform under pressure. In-person job interviews are stressful situations, especially if you are expected to present in front of a group. Your potential employer will be watching to see how you hold up when all eyes are on you.

Another key aspect that your potential future employer will be assessing, even if not in an overt way, is your emotional intelligence—that is, how well you can read a room. For example, an interviewer might notice whether you pick up social cues from those you are speaking with or whether you can engage strangers in comfortable conversation.

It is also not uncommon for on-site interviews for alt-ac positions to include a form of authentic assessment of your skills and abilities. For example, we authors have hired employees who have been asked to create marketing materials during a specific time limit, facilitate a workshop on a topic of the candidate's choice, or complete a mock consultation with a faculty client who was observed by the search committee.

You may also be asked to offer a workshop, present on a topic (and it will most likely *not* be your dissertation research), offer advice on a challenge or problem, or do something else that provides the interviewers some other way of assessing how your skills and experience relate to the job for which you are interviewing. As you prepare for an on-site alt-ac interview, consider this additional advice.

Know Whom You Will Meet

It is not uncommon for alt-ac job interviews to involve multiple meetings with different groups throughout the day. If you are not provided with a detailed agenda that includes the names and position titles of whom you will be meeting with, consider asking for this information at least a week before your interview.

Know Your Questions

For each group that you meet with, you will probably be asked what questions you have for its members. Consider developing a list of questions for the hiring manager (i.e., questions about their vision for the unit, information about how the position came to be, etc.), a human resources representative (i.e., questions about salary range, benefits, etc.), peers whom you will be working with (i.e., questions about a typical day, the workplace culture, what they like about working there, etc.), and any other group that you know you will be meeting with.

Be Prepared

You may be talking for extended periods of time, especially if you have meetings with multiple teams or people in one day. Bring a bottle of water and an energy bar to keep your throat clear and your energy levels high.

Arrive Early

If you are traveling to your interview location, try to arrive at a decent time the day before your interview so that you can get a good night's sleep the night before and not feel rushed in any last-minute preparations or practicing that you want to complete before the big day.

Expect the Best, but Plan for the Worst

Going into your interview optimistic is a key element to a successful on-site visit, but you should also plan for technology failures and other mishaps that can cause a hiccup in your plans. Make sure to bring all the technology you need, store a backup of any presentations (and send them to the interview site in advance), and preprint any documents you plan to provide at the interview. All kinds of things can happen on interview day, and you want to stay as calm as possible. Backup plans keep you from getting flustered if you encounter any challenges.

Take Notes

Throughout the day, try to note the main questions you are asked and the people whom you talk with. Once the day is over, you'll find that you do not remember a thing. The notes can help you reflect on how things went and can assist you if you decide to debrief the day with family members or colleagues. Noting the names of the people whom you talk with throughout the interview will help you follow up with brief thank-you notes.

Follow Up With Thank-You Notes

You saw this one coming, right? Because job searches can happen very rapidly, and you probably will not know if you are the first or last candidate being interviewed, we recommend immediately following up with thank-you e-mails after your visit. All members of the search committee and anyone whom you met with individually throughout the day should be contacted. Try to write these notes the night of your interview or early the following morning, because you don't know when decisions about candidates will be made.

Next Steps

Put yourself in the shoes of the person on the other side of the interview table. If you were interviewing someone for a job, what are the kinds of things that you would be looking for? Confidence, clear responses, and specific examples are just a few of the universal things that people might be looking for in a job candidate. When we interviewed potential employees in the past, we also always looked for people who are interested in helping solve the organization's problems. By looking at the interview process from your potential employer's perspective, you might be able to bring something unique to the table.

Want to take your interview skills to the next level? We recommend practicing some of your interview answers and recording yourself with either audio or video so that you can review your responses. Although it can be awkward to listen to or watch yourself, this is one of the best ways to see how others will see you in the interview. Most computers come with built-in software for audio and video recording (QuickTime is a good example), so no extra equipment is needed. The best part? You can get all of your stumbles out of the way before the real thing.

PART FOUR

ADDRESSING COMMON ALT-AC CHALLENGES

P art Four covers common challenges for people pursuing alt-ac careers. We share strategies for managing the expectations that the people closest to you have about your career. If you and your partner are looking for academic and/or alt-ac positions at the same time—also known as the "two-body problem"—this part will help you find ways to avoid one of you having to give up your dreams. We also give you ideas for finding niche areas in which to develop expertise and an audience for your work. This part helps you explore ways to leverage the work you did for your dissertation, converting it into other, more visible formats. We share advice about establishing credibility and a reputation. Last, we give instructions to set up and facilitate effective conversations with people who can give you career advice or help you get into an alt-ac position.

14

ADDRESSING THE
TWO-BODY PROBLEM

In this chapter, you will (a) compare different versions of the two-body problem and (b) examine how geographic location affects the equation.

Different Versions of the Same Problem

Are you and your partner both working in or seeking academic and/or alt-ac positions? At the same time? When one of you is already working at a higher education institution? While one of you finishes your graduate work? These are variations of the dual-career challenge or two-body problem. Matt Reed (2013) described the *two-body problem* as "an inelegant term for the difficulty that couples have in finding good jobs for both people that are geographically close enough that they can continue to live together" (para. 1). No matter what you call it, the challenge is real. Solving the challenge can mean one person or both people giving up a dream job, as well as the couple temporarily living apart and making hard choices about having children. Our goal is to help you find solutions that avoid negative consequences of the two-body problem, to the extent possible.

Two People Working in or Seeking Academic Positions

The dual-career challenge is more common than you might think. In a 2015 *Scientific American* survey of almost 1,600 people, "89 percent had experienced or expected to experience the two-body problem" (Harrington, 2015, para. 2). Over 3,000 people had responded to the same survey the year before, with similar results—90% had faced, were facing, or felt they would face the two-body problem in their past, present, or future (Giller, 2014). A more recent study of over 2,000 respondents across 7 universities found that for almost 65% of them, "both [partners] wanted to find faculty positions at the time of hire" at their current institution (Zhang & Kmec, 2018, p. 770).

Respondents to both *Scientific American* surveys felt that location, income, and prestige—in that order—were the top factors that played a role in deciding if one partner should follow the other. Also, in all 3 surveys, very few people reported being able to find jobs at the same institution; Zhang and Kmec (2018) found that fewer than 15% were hired together. In 2015, over two-thirds of the respondents would be willing to live apart for 7 years or more if both could have their dream jobs. Half would be willing to live apart but within driving distance; a third would be willing to live within flying distance in the same part of the country. These statistics speak to how difficult it can be for 2 people to pursue individual career goals as a couple, even when both have put considerable time and effort into their own preparation.

McNeil and Sher (2001) conducted their own dual-career-couple survey of 620 members of the American Physical Society in 1998, identifying factors that affect career and life decisions and listing potential outcomes. Factors that played a role in the couple's decisions included being in the same or different fields, being in similar or different stages in their careers, and desiring to have children or not.

Potential outcomes for couples in physics and related STEM disciplines include shared or split tenure-track positions for couples who are in the same field, dual hiring, one or both people taking alt-ac positions or nonacademic positions, or the couple living in different cities. McNeil and Sher (2001) recognized additional challenges for women, who were more likely to be slightly younger than their partner or spouse, which in most cases also meant at earlier stages in their graduate studies or careers.

In a larger study of dual-career academic couples, Schiebinger, Henderson, and Gilmartin (2008) surveyed over 9,000 full-time faculty participants at 13 research universities. Of the respondents, 36% had academic partners, and 36% had partners employed in nonacademic positions. Their results pointed to some hopeful trends on the institutional side. For example, dual hires increased from 3% in the 1970s to 13% in the 2000s. Schiebinger and colleagues made policy recommendations that would support even more dual hires, and we hope more institutions adopt them. Longtime administrator Matt Reed (2018) posited that despite these gains, "the two-body problem is a hiring problem" (para. 6).

Five of the aforementioned studies found that dual hiring, while on the rise, is still rare—only 10% to 15% of respondents in each study reported being offered positions at the same institution. Visiting or temporary faculty positions, including working as an adjunct, and soft money research positions can offer couples temporary options to work together but ultimately are not a solution (McNeil & Sher, 2001; Reed, 2018).

McNeil and Sher (2001) described shared or split positions for two people with degrees in the same field. In a shared position, "a single faculty position is shared by two individuals" (para. 2). In a split position, each person is offered a half-time position. These solutions are creative, but both you and your partner may just want a full position. Dual-career assistance programs offer more options, especially if you pursue positions in a metropolitan area that has several higher education institutions. We discuss these two strategies in more detail later in this chapter.

Looking at individuals, the large study showed that women were more likely to feel that both careers are equal, making their partner's work situation and opportunities a key factor in their own decisions about careers. Schiebinger and colleagues (2008) found that "not only do women more often men perceive a loss in professional mobility as a result of their academic partnerships (54% for women versus 41% for men), but they actively refuse job offers if their partner cannot find a satisfactory position" (p. 4). When Melati Nungsari and her husband moved to Malaysia to pursue their only joint-hire opportunity—after a year of living in different parts of the country while raising a toddler—her Indiana colleagues collectively shared something they had kept hidden: "Women generally seem to feel more pressured than men to give up their professional ambitions for the sake of the family" (Nungsari, 2017, para. 20).

One Person Seeking an Academic Position, One Person Seeking an Alt-Ac Position

At the beginning of this book, we discussed the challenge caused by the diminishing number of tenure-track faculty positions. A variety of academics and alt-acs have written articles and more personal stories about the topic, often emphasizing the difficulties women face in dual-career scenarios. One blog author using a pseudonym, Lazuli (2014), chronicled her experiences with the two-body problem and credits it for her decision to pursue alt-ac positions in digital and academic libraries instead of tenure-track positions in history and religious studies.

Michelle Parrinello-Cason (2012) challenged assumptions that she and other women "sell themselves short" (para. 14) for pursuing positions other than tenure-track positions at universities. Kelly Baker (2014b) testified to her computational science husband's commitment to take positions in industry, government, or academia to support her tenure-track job search in religious studies. However, this was countered by gender inequity during academic interviews: Baker (2014a, 2014b) described herself and other women being asked about their husbands, but men not being asked about their wives. Lauren Rivera (2017) found the same gender inequalities and relationship status discrimination in academic hiring at a large Research-1 Carnegie Classification (R1) university.

Same-sex couples often face a narrower field of options. Issues to consider include whether to work at institutions "in states where legislation prevents offering benefits to unmarried couples, which, in effect, blocks active hiring of same-sex partners" and whether the couple must be "out" before negotiating a dual hire (Schiebinger et al., 2008, p. 12). Alex Bond (2013) wrote about the challenge of living and working in Canada, which has progressive same-sex marriage rights but only 100 or so higher education institutions. Before the 2015 U.S. Supreme Court ruling to legalize same-sex marriage, Bond and his husband did not consider seeking positions in the United States—which has almost 4,500 colleges and universities—because of immigration and equality challenges.

Two People Working in or Seeking Alt-Ac Positions

So far we have described the two-body problem by looking only at different couple combinations. The authors at *Scientific American* noted that to solve the two-body problem in classical mechanics or physics, you use equations to determine the trajectories of two bodies orbiting each other over time, but first you need their initial positions and initial velocities (Giller, 2014; Harrington, 2015). While we don't have a set of equations for you, we do have some ideas to help you make decisions if you find yourself in the same situation.

Let's look at a couple where both individuals hold alt-ac positions. Charity Peak is a regional director of academic programs for the Association of College and University Educators (ACUE). Before taking on her current role, she worked as the director of faculty development at the U.S. Air Force Academy, where she had taught for six years. After working as a principal at two schools and a district HR director, her husband, David, is now the assistant superintendent for human resources at a school district in Colorado Springs. Charity Peak told us about their biggest challenges with the two-body problem—for starters, they pursued PhD programs at the same time, while they also had young children—and how they have addressed those challenges:

When you're both at that same level, you can understand each other's pain. The divorce rate is high [among dual-career academics], so there's something to be said for commiserating. Always, it's about keeping your mind on the end goal, whatever that looks like for you, trying to be gracious. It's truly a selfish act [to get a PhD]. You're spending time, money, and energy that you cannot spend on anything else.

My goal with getting the PhD was to both advance my career and have flexibility for family. Originally, my intent was to be a professor at a university—professors have a little flexibility when they can come and go. The problem is, I also wanted to be in a leadership capacity. And then you lose that flexibility, as staff positions require regular hours. I wish academia—other than your teaching—better accommodated the idea of flexibility around families.

It's really hard for both partners to excel and also have a family. David's job is locked down, so we chose to have me be more flexible. I was a scatter plot—always in education but guided by what my daughters need rather than my personal career. I love teaching, which is what drew me to professional development. I ended up at the Air Force Academy—which is strict—to be in a teaching and learning center. That's what drew me to doing my own consulting. I wanted to have a professional capacity. I like to geek out about stuff, but my daughter had a [health-related emergency] and priorities shifted.

The benefit about ACUE for me is I'm able to work from home. Before ACUE, I had turned down four different job offers. I kept my vision alive regarding what I wanted my life to look like. My income is a bonus, so I had the luxury of being able to do that. That is a gift not everybody has.

I really hope that people can stay committed to whatever their dream is and achieve it. I think if you're a teacher, there's a lot of different ways to leverage being a teacher—if people can expand their mind beyond having a faculty position. Having a PhD shows your level of tenacity more than your level of intellect. It's about opening your mind to what the possibilities are. (C. Peak, personal communication, June 19, 2018)

Location, Location, Location

Veteran alt-ac Ruth Nemire's first piece of advice to people pursing alt-ac or academic careers is "You should always love where you live" (R. Nemire, personal communication, February 1, 2018). The *Scientific American* surveys confirmed that location plays one of the largest roles in career decisions, regardless of which couple combination resonates with you. Schiebinger and colleagues (2008) found that

> major universities in relatively isolated settings, such as small college towns, have a great need to accommodate couples, whereas institutions in metropolitan areas can sometimes successfully offer faculty to neighboring universities or at least expect that the partner will be able to find employment in the area. (p. 67)

We will focus on the opportunities you might find in metropolitan areas (see Table 14.1). If you search the Internet for metropolitan areas with the most colleges and universities, you get varying results including lists of the "most educated cities," "best college cities for students," "cities with the most college students," and "cities that host the most universities that appear in the *U.S. News* rankings." While these are all interesting statistics, they can be misleading. Knowing the metro areas that actually have the most institutions of higher education gives you a better chance of finding two academic and/ or alt-ac jobs within driving distance from where you live.

You can find the number of colleges near most cities in the United States using the Nearest Colleges tool provided by College Simply (www.college simply.com/colleges-near) or searching Wikipedia for "colleges and universities in metropolitan _____." When you and your partner are choosing a location for the next stage of your lives together, other factors to consider (in no particular order) include, but are not limited to, proximity to your family, friends, and extended support network; the cost of living; the cost and availability of housing; traffic patterns and public transportation options; the quality of schools; and even annual weather patterns. If you have children, see the tool offered by the *New York Times* to find good schools and affordable homes in five metropolitan areas: New York, San Francisco, Boston, Chicago, and Minneapolis (www.nytimes.com/interactive/2017/03/30/ upshot/good-schools-affordable-homes-suburban-sweet-spots.html).

Next Steps

During your job searches, search the websites of institutions you are considering using terms such as *dual career, relocation,* or *spousal hiring*. For example, you can find dual-career assistance programs at a variety of institutions, including the following:

- The University of Wisconsin–Madison (facstaff.provost.wisc.edu/ dual-career-couple-assistance-program)
- Purdue University (www.purdue.edu/provost/faculty/resources/dual Career.html)
- Missouri State (www.missouristate.edu/provost/dualcareerpgm.htm)

TABLE 14.1

Metropolitan Areas With High Numbers of Colleges and Universities as of December 2018

Metropolitan Area	Number of Colleges and Universities in Metro Area[a]	Average Home Prices in Metro Area (as of March 2018)[b]	Cost of Living Without Rent (for Four-Person Family)[c]	Average Annual Temperatures (Average, High, and Low)[d]
Atlanta	50 within 50 miles	$190,000	$3,291.64 (rank 79 out of 447 world cities)	Avg: 62.6°F High: 71.9°F Low: 53.2°F
Boston	53 total	$398,000	$3,752.54 (rank 24 out of 447)	Avg: 51.4°F High: 58.7°F Low: 44.1°F
Chicago	107	$218,000	$3,559.30 (rank 35 out of 447)	Avg: 51.3°F High: 59.3°F Low: 43.3°F
Los Angeles	100 in LA County	$605,000	$3,639.68 (rank 33 out of 447)	Avg: 63.8°F High: 71.7°F Low: 55.9°F
New York	115	$425,000	$4,609.02 (rank 10 out of 447)	Avg: 55.2°F High: 62.3°F Low: 48.0°F

(*Continues*)

TABLE 14.1 (*Continued*)

Metropolitan Area	Number of Colleges and Universities in Metro Area[a]	Average Home Prices in Metro Area (as of March 2018)[b]	Cost of Living Without Rent (for Four-Person Family)[c]	Average Annual Temperatures (Average, High, and Low)[d]
Philadelphia	80 + 94 within 50 miles	$190,000	$3,598.95 (rank 30 out of 447)	Avg: 55.9°F High: 64.7°F Low: 47.0°F
San Francisco	98 total: 34 public, 49 private, 15 seminaries	$750,000	$4,199.02 (rank 15 out of 447)	Avg: 57.3°F High: 63.8°F Low: 50.8°F
Washington DC	20 in DC + 58 within 50 miles	$375,000	$4,388.23 (rank 14 out of 447)	Avg: 55.7°F High: 64.8°F Low: 46.6°F

[a]College Simply (www.collegesimply.com/colleges-near) and Wikipedia (e.g., en.wikipedia.org/wiki/List_of_colleges_and_universities_in_metropolitan_Atlanta, en.wikipedia.org/wiki/List_of_colleges_and_universities_in_the_San_Francisco_Bay_Area, en.wikipedia.org/wiki/List_of_colleges_and_universities_in_metropolitan_Boston).

[b]Average home prices: Kiplinger (www.kiplinger.com/tool/real-estate/T010-S003-home-prices-in-100-top-u-s-metro-areas/index.php).

[c]Cost of living: Numbeo (www.numbeo.com/cost-of-living).

[d]Annual weather averages: U.S. Climate Data (www.usclimatedata.com).

If your partner is seeking or working in a tenure-track position, these offices will help you seek faculty or alt-ac positions on campus, as well as academic, alt-ac, and non-ac positions in the surrounding community or region.

You'll find a comprehensive list of dual-career programs on the HERC website (www.hercjobs.org/career_advice/Dual-Careers/campuses_with_dual_Career_programs/index.html). You can also download the Dual Career Toolkit from Stanford University's Clayman Institute for Gender Research (gender .stanford.edu/publications/dual-career-toolkit). The toolkit provides tips for applicants at different stages of the hiring process.

15

FINDING A NICHE AND AN APPROPRIATE AUDIENCE

In this chapter, you will identify the need and strategies for finding a niche and an appropriate audience, based on a variety of goals (e.g., personal and professional, short term and long term).

To Niche or Not to Niche?

If you've had to write, or will be writing, a dissertation, you probably know that many people start with a topic they are passionate about, then conduct a literature review to unearth gaps in the literature. Hiding in those gaps are questions that have not yet been answered and opportunities to make unique contributions to the ever-growing knowledge base of your discipline. In the professional world of alt-ac, it is possible to go through a similar process to find a niche for yourself to meet needs that have not yet been met and make unique contributions to your institution, your field, or both.

Ask yourself if you need or want a niche. That niche might be one aspect of your daily work that you develop more than any other area. You might do this out of personal or professional interest, to meet a need at your workplace, or to gain skills necessary for another position later in your career. Then again, you may not see a need for a niche—now or at any time in the future—and that's okay, too.

Michael Wing has proven that alt-ac professionals can create their own niche, on their own terms. Wing (2017) recently published *Passion Projects for Smart People*, in which he described "how to do serious intellectual work in your spare time—and turn side projects into career-building opportunities" (https://quilldriverbooks.com/products-page-2/business/passion-projects-for-smart-people/). Having started on the tenure track, he decided not to pursue tenure because of uncertainty about the availability of faculty positions during an economic downturn. However, Wing now feels that "you can have all the best things of being a professor without having to be one" (M. Wing, personal communication, February 1, 2018).

Wing describes himself as a generalist rather than a specialist and enjoys the idea of "owning everything in science and not going super deep on one small thing" (M. Wing, personal communication, February 1, 2018). As a full-time teacher at Sir Francis Drake High School, Wing has continued to publish papers—some with his high school students—pursue grants, and write books. His niche has been to pursue intellectual projects in the sciences that are original and "at the edge of human knowledge" (M. Wing, personal communication, February 1, 2018). While the numbers don't support a tenure-track job for everyone, he advises doctoral students to "get a 'real job'—permanent, stable, with benefits—and . . . build yourself an academic life that's just as rewarding" (M. Wing, personal communication, February 1, 2018).

There are examples of both needing and not needing niches in many fields. In medicine, for example, you might decide to become a general practitioner who treats almost anyone for whatever health issues they present. On the other hand, you might choose to pursue a specialty requiring special skills, like surgery; serving an age group, like pediatrics; or focusing on one part of the body, like psychiatry. If it looks like there are too many people working in or pursuing the same specialty, you can pick another specialty or dive deeper into a subspecialty such as complex general surgical oncology, pediatric critical care medicine, or addiction psychiatry.

In the example of higher education professional development, you might decide to work for a Center for Teaching and Learning and support almost any faculty member with whatever pedagogical issues that person presents. On the flip side, you might choose to pursue a specialty requiring special skills, like distance education; serving a discipline group, like medical educators; or focusing on one part of the instructional process, like assessment. In this case, there is often room to do both—work for a faculty development center and focus a percentage of your efforts on a specific audience or challenge. Again, this may depend on the level of need at your institution for specializing in certain areas. If you feel strongly about pursuing a specialty, you might need to present your case to your manager or develop yourself on your own time.

Before we leave the question of needing a niche, let's look at some of the pros and cons. If you see yourself wanting to deliver conference presentations, publish articles or books, or facilitate workshops for other institutions as a consultant, then having one or more specialties will be important. You will want to become known for your expertise and/or research in an area that excites you, so your name is the first on other people's minds when they need help in that area.

Conversely, developing expertise in a specific area requires more time; for example, surgical residencies last at least five years compared to pediatric residencies, which usually last three. Moreover, maintaining expertise often means continuing self-education. In the professional development example, the technologies used for distance education constantly evolve, so practitioners constantly must learn to use new tools and teaching strategies. Ultimately, having additional skills benefits you in many ways, so if now is not a good time, consider finding a niche at a future stage of your career.

Finding the Right Niche for You

You have not skipped to the next chapter, so hopefully you have decided to find your niche now rather than later. Where should you begin? Let's look at the story of Lee Skallerup Bessette, an alt-ac professional who, by day, works as a learning design specialist at Georgetown University. Skallerup Bessette also acts as an academic coach, a writer, and a social media consultant. Part of a dual academic couple, she took on the role of the trailing spouse and found herself in a contingent faculty position. She had gotten her PhD because she loved teaching and wanted to make a difference in the classroom. After she gave a tenure-track position one more go, a colleague suggested she would be great at faculty development. She saw it as an opportunity to make a broader difference at the institution and to help make institutional change.

To find her niche, Skallerup Bessette started by conducting a skills assessment. She went to the career center to find the right tools to do a skills inventory: "What am I known for?" This inventory focused on listing, so she started listing everything she could imagine. She threw everything at the wall to see what would stick. Ultimately, she found social media as a niche, but she did not go into that area just for the sake of being on social media. At first, she had just wanted to connect—being in a geographically isolated location, she began to engage in social media.

She also has a lot of varied interests and wanted to find academics and educators, so she followed hashtags on Twitter and did some informational interviews. Like Skallerup Bessette found, doing informational interviews and exploring the Internet can also help you find those gaps in the field and who currently fills them. Who is writing, speaking, or doing something in the alt-ac space around you? Just as important, ask "What aren't they doing?" to find gaps within gaps.

Veterans often share short sets of questions or tenets to help emerging practitioners find their niche in a variety of fields, such as leadership (J. Miller, n.d.) or entrepreneurship (Boss, 2015). From those sets there are a number of common themes and questions that will work for finding your alt-ac niche, too. We developed some questions to guide you through your process.

First, set your starting point through your values, your strengths, and your passions. What are your core values and areas of strength?

_____

_____

_____

Building from that list of strengths, what brings you joy and/or ignites your passion?

_____

_____

_____

Next, plot a course toward a niche based on what distinguishes you, along with your goals and others' unmet needs. What makes you unique?

_____

_____

_____

What are your most relevant personal or professional goals?

_____

_____

_____

What do people at your institution or in your field need?

_____

_____

_____

After that, scan the environment to find who is working in the areas you've identified. Who is writing, speaking, or doing something in the alt-ac space around you, and what are they known for?

What aren't they doing?

Last, as Chiuri (2012) pointed out, your niche may actually be outside your comfort zone. Finalize your niche destination with what risks you are willing to take. What is worth taking risks?

If you plan on publishing or consulting, what will people pay for?

Going back to Skallerup Bessette's story, she had always been curious about technology in teaching. She feels lucky she had the space and time to experiment with social media, as well as blogging and coaching. She started exploring what she was good at, what she could do, and what she liked about higher education. She actually had two ideas of where to go—faculty development just came together faster than university relations and public relations, which she liked because of the work involving social media and writing, one of her biggest strengths.

Another strength came from an unexpected source. Skallerup Bessette had always discounted that she coached swimming, but she found that skill has been important in other alt-ac roles, telling people how to do something technically. She felt teaching should be more like coaching—"I can't swim for them!"—and helping learners make corrections. When she described the skills assessment process, she explained, "When I coach technical corrections in swimming, physical manipulation of body, I need to do it in different ways (analogies, demo, description)" (L. Skallerup Bessette, personal communication, February 6, 2018). It is a strategy she had inadvertently developed. In other words, explaining concepts in different ways is a skill she got from coaching swimming more than from teaching.

As a result, she advises people considering alt-ac careers not to discount hobbies and other interests. Those networks can be invaluable in finding positions outside of academia. She gave the example of her husband's friend from his doctoral program, who now works as a consultant. His job came from networking at judo classes. Her moral: You don't know who the person will be to let you through the door—someone at judo, in a knitting circle, or volunteering at an animal shelter. Make time for hobbies and interests outside of school, partly because they may generate interesting leads.

Finding and Growing Your Audience or Community

Once you have found a niche or two, it is time to find an audience. Some of you might be asking why you would need or want an audience. Education attracts altruistic people, so you may want to make contributions to your field. For example, you might want to share your most recent research findings. Others see having an audience as being part of a community, where sharing is reciprocal. Michelle Miller (2018) characterized an audience as being a fan base that can provide "feedback that shows your work reached people in the way you intended" (para. 10) and "spread the word about your work" (para. 12). Giving back to your chosen community might also mean showing others how to use a teaching technique that has proven to increase student success. At some point, you may want to become a public speaker, an author, or a consultant, where having an audience adds considerable value.

Professional organizations, associations, and societies are a good place to start. Often these organizations will have online discussion groups, electronic mailing lists, or other public forums that allow you to reach and connect with others. As you gain expertise in your niche areas, you will be able to answer questions, share resources that you have used or created, or point people to your work in other ways.

Colleagues at sibling institutions are another audience or community. For example, your institution may belong to a larger system, such as a two-year college in a district or statewide system; a campus that was established to serve a specific population, like historically Black colleges and universities; a university that belongs to an umbrella organization, like the Association of Public and Land-grant Universities (APLU); or a research lab that is 1 of

17 national laboratories funded by the U.S. Department of Energy. Within these systems, you may also belong to 1 or more system-wide groups or committees.

These work-related groups may lead to opportunities for professional growth. For example, Kevin Kelly, one of the authors of this book, had created a workshop for faculty at his institution, San Francisco State University, about universal design for online learning—applying universal design for learning (UDL) concepts to online teaching and learning. He mentioned his workshop when the same topic was raised at a system-wide meeting of academic technology directors and managers.

Soon after that meeting, a colleague at Sacramento State University invited him to deliver the workshop at the summer institute Teachers Using Technology. Kelly took a day off, drove to Sacramento, and conducted the workshop, which was a big success. Since then, Kelly has progressively woven his UDL work into conference presentations, peer-reviewed journal articles, an online course for Lynda.com, workshops facilitated as a consultant, and a book about inclusive online teaching.

From this story, we see that finding your audience can start with and through people you know, but it can also grow over time with a combination of strategy, hard work, and taking advantage of opportunities that come your way. Conferences in your field are filled with potential audience members and can lead to additional opportunities to share your niche expertise. Your network will act as nodes within your larger audience, helping make connections to new audience members and potential work. For example, a colleague consultant and author knew about one of Kelly's niches and recommended him as a workshop facilitator for a community college.

Social media platforms and blogs make it possible to build an audience virtually. For Skallerup Bessette, blogging became "hiding in plain sight"— no one at her institution ever noticed her work, but she had quickly gained a large following online. If you decide to write a blog, you might focus the majority of your initial writing about your niche area to attract like-minded people who face the same challenges. Blogs, electronic portfolios, and personal websites also provide opportunities to aggregate your work when your audience wants to see more of your work.

Once you become known for your niche area, popular organizations may ask you to write a guest post—or you can approach them to solicit interest. With their large base of readers, these organizations can help you increase your own audience reach. Over time, you also may develop several niche areas. In Derek Bruff's blog *Agile Learning* (derekbruff.org), the primary navigation showcases some of his niche areas—backchannels, clickers, and visual thinking. The secondary navigation lists over two dozen areas that interest him. At some point, you may want to become a public speaker, an author, or a consultant. A virtual presence will help you gain audience members for these activities.

To help you think about your audience, we provided some additional questions. To what systems does your institution belong? What groups or committees can you join to connect with colleagues at sibling institutions?

_____

_____

_____

To what associations and/or societies do you belong? Which conferences do you attend?

_____

_____

_____

What journals and/or sources of online articles do you read regularly?

_____

_____

_____

Next Steps

If you haven't done so already, answer the questions presented in this chapter related to finding your niche area(s) and finding your audience. You will find that one often leads to the other! There is a reason why conferences regularly offer "birds of a feather" sessions for people to connect with others who play similar roles or solve similar problems at their respective places of work. Take the information you developed here, refer back to the alt-ac career trajectory you mapped in chapter 6, and consider these questions:

- Do the niche areas you identified help you reach career milestones, or will they distract you from reaching your personal and professional goals?

- Does thinking about growing your audience make you want to add consulting, public speaking, publishing, or another skill set to your career map?

If you are ready to do more work in these areas, see some of the related topics we cover in more detail in later chapters; for example, chapter 23, "Joining and Participating in Professional Organizations," and chapter 27, "Creating and Growing a Personal Brand."

16

COMMUNICATING HOW DISCIPLINARY KNOWLEDGE AND SKILLS SUPPORT WORK IN SPECIFIC ALT-AC ROLES

In this chapter, you will translate your disciplinary knowledge and academic skills to different alt-ac careers (e.g., professional development, research, technology, etc.).

Making Relevant Connections Between Your Past and Your Future

Depending on the career pathway you have chosen, there will be varying levels of direct relationship between the training you received in your discipline and your current role. Knowing how to leverage your disciplinary training for a successful alt-ac career is an important skill set to have as you progress along your career pathway. Plus, at some point during your alt-ac career, someone will inquire about your original disciplinary field of study, and it's nice to be able to draw a map of how you got from there to here. In this chapter, we'll offer some ideas about how to connect your disciplinary skills to your alt-ac career when you have a more indirect pathway between the two, as well as when you can see direct connections between your training and your alt-ac role.

Indirect Connections Between Your Disciplinary Training and Your Alt-Ac Role

Sometimes, when you begin to pursue an alt-ac career path, you take a bit of a left turn from where you originally started in your disciplinary training. However, even if your discipline seems a bit far removed from what you are

105

currently doing, we would wager that there are more connections than you might think. Here's a specific example of the skills that have translated from Linder's original discipline of women's and gender studies to her work in faculty development and research on teaching and learning in higher education. Women's and gender studies

- is an interdisciplinary field—faculty development involves working with faculty from a range of disciplines;
- involves training in the theories and practice of advocacy—faculty development often involves serving as an advocate for faculty to upper administration;
- involves research via qualitative methods such as interviews and focus groups (among others)—skills that Linder has used in her research in faculty development and in the scholarship of teaching and learning;
- is a field that merges theory with practice—Linder has used this skill throughout her work in higher education and her research on faculty development, online teaching and learning, and student experiences in the classroom;
- emphasizes the importance of women's voices—Linder has worked to develop her own voice as a public speaker and author throughout her career as a researcher and consultant; and
- values critical pedagogies in the classroom—Linder has used her prior research on critical pedagogies in her current research on educational theory and practice.

This list offers a range of examples of how Linder can leverage the skills and knowledge she picked up in her disciplinary training in her current alt-ac role. Moreover, she has been able to strengthen her alt-ac skills and abilities by relying on her previous disciplinary training and allowing that training to be infused into her current work.

As you begin to think about the different ways that you might translate your disciplinary knowledge and skills into an alt-ac role, here are some questions to help you identify the abilities you have that are unique to you and your training:

- What discipline-specific skills did you learn related to research methodology and design?
- What are the foundational components of your discipline? Can you translate any of your discipline-specific knowledge into more generalized settings?

- What are the foundational components of any subdisciplines that you studied? Can you translate any of your discipline-specific knowledge into more generalized settings?
- Did you learn any particular technology-related skills (specific computer programs, software or hardware skills, etc.) during your disciplinary training?
- What other skills did you learn (i.e., teamwork, collaboration, project management, etc.) that might be applicable to your alt-ac work?

These questions may help you identify some new areas that you had not considered as possibilities that translate well from your discipline to your alt-ac career.

Once you have answered each of these questions with a list of different skills and abilities that you have, we recommend trying to come up with concrete examples of those areas of expertise. These concrete examples are useful for the cover letters and interview situations that we discussed in Part Three, as well as for situations when you are asked to explain your career pathway to others who are interested in how you got to where you are today.

Direct Connections Between Your Disciplinary Training and Your Alt-Ac Role

Some alt-ac professionals have a more direct pathway between their disciplinary training and their alt-ac role. For example, John Whitmer, who became interested in learning analytics while serving as an academic administrator, got his doctorate in education while working in that role. This project garnered the interest of Blackboard, a learning management software company, and he was asked to lead their internal research and development using learning analytics—applying his academic skills with a very large data set and immediate impact in the products the company creates. It may be that you are still interested in working directly with the knowledge and skills of your discipline, but you just don't see yourself pursuing a tenure-track role. Or perhaps you enjoy your discipline, but you don't enjoy a particular aspect of faculty life, such as research or teaching. If this is the case for you, we recommend that you start by asking yourself the following questions:

- What about your discipline are you particularly passionate about? What could you happily focus on for the next 5 to 10 years?
- What about your discipline are you less passionate about? What would feel like a relief if you never had to do it again?

- What are your areas of strength within your discipline? What are you good at?
- What are your areas of weakness within your discipline? What are you challenged by?

These questions can get you started with identifying and narrowing down the particular areas that you might want to pursue in an alt-ac career. (Keep in mind, even if something is an area of weakness or challenge, you can and should pursue it if it happens to be of interest to you.)

Once you have answered these questions, start brainstorming all of the different career path offshoots from your discipline. One way to do this is to look at the different jobs that alums from your department have taken. Another method is to create a visual map of how your discipline relates to different fields and industries outside of higher education. Consider various relationships to the following areas and industries:

- Software or website development
- Health-care or wellness industries
- Publishing
- Community nonprofits or nonprofit foundations
- Public education
- Art, museums, and theater
- Finance
- Coaching or consulting

This is certainly not an exhaustive list of all of the places where you might be able to connect your disciplinary training to outside fields or industries, but it can serve as a starting point to generating your own list. Begin by taking each one of these items and brainstorming all of the different ways that you might connect your disciplinary training to that area. Get creative and don't reject any ideas just yet; this exercise is about putting all of your ideas on the table. Once you have gone through each area (and added your own items), then you can start to narrow things down to the realistic possibilities for you.

What If I Don't Like My Discipline Anymore?

Ah, perhaps you don't really *want* to connect your discipline with your next career step. We get it, and we actually hear this all the time. It's possible that studying your discipline for all of those years has turned you off it completely. This is something that Wapnick (2017) discussed in her book *How to Be Everything*. As we mentioned in chapter 6, Wapnick described what she termed a *multipotentialite*, or a person who likes to do lots of different kinds of things throughout a career. Because of their shifting interests, multipotentialites are prone to not completing advanced degrees, especially doctorates, because they lose interest and want to move on to something else.

If you identify as a multipotentialite, or if you are just tired of your discipline and want to move on to something else, here are some questions that might be useful:

- What are your hobbies? What are the things that you like to devote time to outside of your disciplinary training or interests?
- What do other people come to you for advice for? What do other people think that you are good at?
- If you get into a flow state where you lose all track of time and just sink into your work, what are you doing when this happens?
- What do you like to read about or watch documentaries about? What topics and subjects are genuinely interesting to you?
- When you picture yourself in your ideal job, what are you doing? (Don't hold back on this one—if it's surfing in the ocean or baking cookies, write it down. No judgment.)

We hope that these questions will help you identify the next steps for your alt-ac career path.

Next Steps

To recap, we recommend the following steps:

- Identify the discipline-specific skills, knowledge, and abilities that you have.
- Think about concrete examples of these areas so that you can talk about them in job materials or with colleagues who ask questions about your career pathway.
- Brainstorm potential connections to other industries or fields outside of higher education that might benefit from your discipline-specific skills, knowledge, and abilities.
- Talk with alums from your department to see how they have leveraged their discipline-specific skills, knowledge, and abilities in a range of fields and industries.

Want to go one level deeper? Research famous people to learn about their formal education and see whether it is different from or the same as what they are doing now for their careers. Here are some of our favorite examples:

- Actor Mayim Bialik, who began acting in childhood and appeared on the science-based sitcom *The Big Bang Theory*, has a PhD in neuroscience.
- Basketball player Shaquille O'Neal earned an EdD.
- Ukrainian boxer Wladimir Klitschko has a PhD in sports science.
- Italian designer Miuccia Prada has a PhD in political science.

Exploring the people whom you admire, either in your discipline or in an industry that interests you, is a great place to start. Checking out memoirs of historical figures is another great place to start.

17

MAKING GOOD USE
OF A DISSERTATION
AFTER GRADUATION

In this chapter, you will explore how to (a) use a dissertation as evidence of your expertise and skills, (b) publish from your dissertation in a range of ways, and (c) mine the dissertation for alt-ac career ideas.

Using a Dissertation as Evidence

In chapter 15, Lee Skallerup Bessette's story offered encouragement for alt-ac professionals to take a broader view of what we can do and to remember that skills gained through graduate programs are transferrable. For example, the very act of completing a dissertation and other long written works shows the ability to engage in complex ideas over time. However, you'll have to make that connection for others. You can use the dissertation itself and publications that stem from it to act as calling cards, showcasing to potential employers your discipline expertise, your ability to conduct research and use specific methodologies, and your capacity to complete long-term projects with multiple phases. You can also share those same written works to establish yourself in a particular niche or to help grow an audience that you identified just a few pages ago.

When describing your disciplinary expertise, we recommend striking a balance between common aspects of your work that nonexperts will recognize and the unique elements that set your dissertation apart from previous research studies. The former provides an entryway for anyone to understand the context of your research. The latter allows you to emphasize innovation, pushing the discipline in new directions and/or addressing unmet needs. Capitalizing on your research skills to convince your boss that your unit should take an evidence-based approach to decision-making or that you should be the one to lead a project evaluating the impact of your unit's efforts within the organization are both potential positive outcomes of leveraging your research experience in an alt-ac role.

Other than your dissertation committee, no one knows your work as well as you. To help you think about your research and final product in a different way, you can start by reviewing your dissertation to identify key words that would help people find it in a search.

Open your dissertation and take a minute to make separate key word lists related to different ways to describe various aspects of it, such as the following:

- Your discipline and subdiscipline: for example, astrobiology, cultural studies, sociology, teaching English as a second language
- Your research methodology: for example, qualitative study, focus group, survey, gas chromatography, astronomical observations, applied research, sentiment analysis of text messages
- Your data analysis technique(s): for example, regression, analysis of variance (ANOVA), topic modeling
- Your research topic: for example, using capsaicin to control peripheral nerve pain
- Your research population, if applicable: for example, higher education students transferring from two-year to four-year institutions
- Aspects of your work that are trending or perpetually popular: for example, data analytics, stem cells, social media, innovation, organizational change, robotics, nanotechnology, anticancer, renewable energy

As you practice describing your work or telling your story, use these key words to create an "elevator pitch" version—that is, be ready to share all of your key points in the time it takes to ride an elevator with someone. If you are in New York City, the average elevator ride is 118 seconds (Hayzlett, 2012), but we recommend keeping it under 30 seconds and conveying the big idea in the first 5 seconds. You can always expand your thoughts when a prospective employer shows interest!

Creating Short-Form Versions of a Dissertation

In a guest blog post for *The Scholarpreneur*, Hamideh Iraj (n.d.) told graduate students how they can turn graduate work like dissertations into a book. She cited Umberto Eco as her role model, "who wrote a novel based on his PhD dissertation and won the Nobel Prize" (Iraj, n.d., para. 2).

While writing a book is a potential outcome for your work (for one of our favorite resources on this topic, see Germano, 2013), we are going to start with shorter end products, such as publishable journal articles and conference presentations.

We recommend that you begin this process by reflecting on your goals for disseminating your dissertation in the diverse range of forms that we will be discussing in this chapter. For example, common goals range from seeking to increase exposure to supporting your career. For tenure-track positions, using the dissertation for publication is a basic expectation, but for many alt-ac positions, publication or research may not be expected or required. That said, having publications can help you at different points along your alt-ac journey.

When you apply for alt-ac positions that require writing and/or research, the publications will give you an advantage over other candidates. As you work in alt-ac positions, publications can provide additional connection points to colleagues, showcase your expertise in a specific area, or support grant proposal applications. If you decide to apply for a faculty position later in your career, publications will be required.

Although we encourage you to milk the dissertation for all it's worth to advance your career, we also acknowledge that sometimes the most important role of the dissertation is to earn you the letters of PhD after your name and that's it. You will have to weigh the work involved against the potential benefits. However you decide to use the ideas in this chapter, starting with a clear goal in mind or, at the very least, a sense of how your dissertation relates to your larger career trajectory can be helpful.

Journal Articles

Through their research, Thomas and Skinner (2012) reviewed the literature about converting dissertations into journal articles and found that there are different approaches, ranging from revising individual dissertation chapters as potential articles to rewriting new articles from scratch. As an end product of this literature review, they created a systematic approach to writing an article based on graduate work.

Their process covers aspects like reviewing the core ideas from your original work and rewriting for a shorter length and a different format. They also give ideas about how to rank and select journals to which you will submit the article for publication. While Belcher (2009) does not address converting dissertations per se, she describes types of academic journal articles, shares common reasons why publications reject submissions, and structures a 12-week process for writing your own article.

As you consider the audience for each potential journal, consider what would be important to them and what background knowledge they would have to have to understand your work. If you conducted a literature review, use some of that information to help your readers understand why your research is important or why it should matter to them. At the same time, you may need to omit major sections of your dissertation that do not work in a new context, rewrite portions in language that is more accessible to newcomers to the field, or both (Gamboa, 2012). Overall, journal articles are shorter, focused pieces, so your job will be to highlight the main findings without reporting all of the results (Thomas & Skinner, 2012, p. 4). Keep an eye on each journal's word limit and contract or expand your ideas to fit the requirements.

In some fields—for example, psychology, economics, science, and engineering—graduate students complete "three-paper" dissertations. This type of dissertation "requires three empirical papers that each make an argument weighty enough to be submitted to a professional journal" (Harvard Department of Psychology, n.d.). The three articles are combined with (a) an introductory chapter that provides context, the theme, and an introduction to the relevant literature and (b) a closing chapter that synthesizes or summarizes the findings. If you followed this dissertation format, then either you have already published or you have submitted a publication to a journal. Consider creating other, short-form versions of your dissertation papers, like conference presentations and/or blog posts, outlined next. If you have not begun your dissertation yet, then check to see if it is an available and appropriate option for you.

Conference Presentations

Conference presentations are another way to expose larger numbers of people to the ideas from your research. In the previous chapter we discussed finding professional organizations that serve your discipline. Look at their websites and review the calls for proposals to present at annual meetings and regional conferences near you. Pay attention to the conference themes, tracks, and special interest groups to identify the greatest overlap with topics from your dissertation.

Before you get too invested, also check the conference registration fees and location. Most conferences require presenters to pay registration fees, which can be expensive. If you are still a graduate student, look for student registration rates. Either way, once you add travel costs, you may find it is too expensive to pursue some opportunities. When you find events that are a good fit for you and your budget, use your key words throughout your proposal's session description. In some cases, the organization will ask you to add key words, too. Check! You already have them.

Once your proposal is accepted, it's time to create a presentation that aligns your work with the conference goals. No matter how long your session is, find ways to engage the participants in activities that make connections to your work. If you have been assigned a poster session, have a common question that you ask each person who stops to talk. For example, "How does my research connect to the work you do?" Use a question to capture the imagination of people who may seem ready to pass you without stopping. If you lead a concurrent session, ask questions to start brief discussions; for example, "Before I start my presentation, what comes to mind when you think of my topic?" or "Before I share my research findings, what do you predict they'll be?"

Blog Posts

You can take small portions of your dissertation and convert them into blog posts, which are more informal than articles and conference presentations. If you do not have a blog or do not intend to start one, contact a popular blog author in your discipline and ask if they would be open to a guest blog post related to some aspect of your research. You can also post on a group blogging platform such as Medium to help people find and share your work. As Hamideh Iraj (n.d.) described earlier, you can always benefit from an established audience that would be interested in what you have to say.

Sharing Dissertation Findings

Tribe and Tunariu (2016) made the point that publishing your research in other formats will widen your audience and exposure. While many dissertations are available through databases like ProQuest, those databases serve only a small percentage of the people who should see your work and ideas. Once you publish a journal article, present at a conference, or even write a blog post, announce it on electronic mailing lists and discussion forums run by professional organizations. Direct the list or discussion participants to your article, a screencast recording of your conference presentation or your write-up in the conference proceedings, or your blog post.

Include more than just a link, of course! Make sure the subject line for your discussion thread or electronic mailing lists message will pique interest. Follow these tips to share your article or blog post via social media platforms, such as LinkedIn or Twitter. Be sure to check with library or law school colleagues about respecting copyright, too (see also Tobin, 2014, as a handy copyright resource).

Sharing on LinkedIn

- Share your journal article, conference presentation, or blog post as a LinkedIn post. Include a graph or chart as an image in the post. Paste the link at the end of the post.
- Consider writing a longer LinkedIn article (i.e., the length of a blog post, or 500 to 750 words) to touch on one aspect of your article or conference presentation. Include a graph or chart from your article as the banner image. Use a question about your topic or statistic from your article as the headline.
- Join LinkedIn Groups (www.linkedin.com/groups [requires having a LinkedIn account]) that serve a specific professional organization, job function, or discipline. Start a conversation in that group to introduce your journal article. Use a question about your topic or statistic from your article as the subject for the conversation to attract readers.
- Regularly check your LinkedIn notifications to learn when people comment on your post or group conversation, so you can reply to them quickly.

Sharing on Twitter

- Use some of your key words as hashtags to attract more clicks to view your article.
- Frame your tweets as a question; for example, "How do #CommunityCollege #transfer #students feel about the transfer process? www. . . ."
- Quote statistics from your dissertation; for example, "Over 1/3 of #students surveyed would be more encouraged to learn a language if they had opportunities to use it outside of the classroom! www. . . ."
- "At-mention" the Twitter handle for a professional association that organizes a conference where you present; for example, "Thanks @AACPharmacy for putting together #PharmEd18! Check out the #LeadershipDevelopment strategies I presented: www. . . ."
- Create a schedule for a small number of follow-up tweets to increase the traffic to your work. Create different versions of your initial tweet to avoid spamming or aggravating your followers.

- Consider making and sharing an infographic version of your research findings. This visualization strategy summarizes your work in an interesting way and will encourage people to review the work behind it. If you have not created infographics before, check out free tools like Piktochart (piktochart.com) and Canva (canva.com), which make it easy to make infographics.

Mining a Dissertation for Alt-Ac Career Ideas

So far in this chapter, we have described methods for you to share your ideas more widely and to create a dialogue with various people, groups, and organizations. It's also possible to use your dissertation to create an internal dialogue. Specifically, you can use your dissertation to generate ideas for alt-ac positions and careers.

If you still have to choose a dissertation topic, then consider topics that may lead to career opportunities—starting with problems that you and your colleagues are trying to solve at work. For example, take our earlier profile on John Whitmer. While working as an academic technology program manager for the California State University system, John began working on projects involving data analytics. He decided to further these questions in a second graduate career, and for his dissertation, he used data analytics techniques to study the relationships among college students' use of the learning management system, the students' characteristics, and their academic achievement (Whitmer, 2013). After earning his degree, Whitmer took a position as Blackboard's director for analytics and research and has since joined ACT, Inc., as a senior director for data science and analytics in its research group. In both of these roles, Whitmer was able to directly continue using the skills he learned in his graduate work and continue in his research interests, while working outside of a traditional academic position. David Perlmutter (2015) asked graduates the question that you can now ask yourself: "How are you using your dissertation to move your career forward?"

In a presentation for graduate students, Barbara Gastel (2013) stated, "The literature review for a dissertation is not just a hurdle to overcome in order to receive a PhD. Rather, both the process and the product serve as foundations to build on in one's career" (p. 6). For example, she advocated becoming familiar with work in your discipline as preparation for research, teaching, policy-making, or consulting. As we did in the previous chapter, she also pointed out the importance of finding unanswered questions in the literature. Those questions are more than dissertation topics. They are research topics for professionals; they are areas of opportunity.

Look through other dissertation sections such as your research methodology to see what jobs or careers might need people with the skills you have. Using key words related to your research approach, conduct a job search on LinkedIn or a job search site. If you loved generating conclusions from your findings, consider a research analyst role. In your calls for future research, identify what opportunities exist to conduct that research yourself—while getting paid! These are just a few examples. Reflect on the aspects of the dissertation process you most enjoyed to find potential alt-ac positions or careers.

Next Steps

Have you decided to share findings from your dissertation more widely? If so, walk through these questions to prepare yourself for the process:

- What are the core ideas you want to share? What format makes the most sense?
- How much time do you have to convert your dissertation into a public-facing format?
- Whom do you want to reach with your ideas? Would that audience understand your dissertation as it is written? If not, how could you convey those same ideas without using specialized language?
- What are your goals behind publishing your work in another format? Do you want to increase your exposure?

If you don't want to publish your dissertation in another format, are there career or job ideas waiting in your work? If this chapter has persuaded you to write an article for publication based on your dissertation or culminating graduate project, two works we mentioned will guide you through a systematic approach:

- Thomas and Skinner (2012) outline a process to convert a dissertation to a journal article, as well as seven rules related to reducing length, providing appropriate descriptions, collaborating with colleagues, following guidelines, and more.
- Belcher (2009) provides a step-by-step process for writing a journal article in 12 weeks (which could be done with content or ideas from your dissertation), including tips for writing cover letters and addressing feedback.

18

ESTABLISHING CREDIBILITY
WHEN GETTING STARTED

In this chapter, you will be presented with (a) information on the importance of reputation in the small world of academia, (b) strategies for establishing credibility as an early-career alt-ac professional, and (c) how to position self-branding and promotion so they are perceived as helpful, not pushy or unseemly.

It Really Is a Small World, After All

Whether you choose to work on a college or university campus or in an alt-ac role outside of a higher education institution, you will quickly learn that professionals know one another and their work. For one thing, academic and alt-ac circles are smaller than many other industries. Furthermore, geographic distances no longer prevent people from seeing each other's work or hearing about colleagues in the field. All it takes is the right person seeing and sharing your journal article or LinkedIn article for it to be seen by dozens, if not hundreds, of potential colleagues.

By extension, as you network with more people and share your work, your reputation may be known widely as well. Imagine tossing a stone into a pond. Your reputation starts within your unit at work, then ripples throughout your organization, various subgroups within your field, and finally the field as a whole (see Figure 18.1). In many ways, this kind of networking and relationship-building is all about creating trust and confidence in you and your work. (We include more information on creating and maintaining a personal brand in chapter 27, so stay tuned.)

Ultimately, you have to ask yourself, how do you want to be known? Write down a few adjectives that you want people to use to describe you and your approach to work or research. If you are just beginning your career journey, potential descriptors might be *collaborative, knowledgeable, professional, strategic, passionate,* or *dedicated*. If you are farther down your career path or you want to project into your own future, additional adjectives might

Figure 18.1. Concentric reputation ripples.

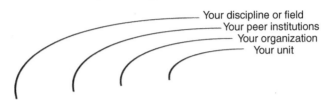

be *experienced, well-connected,* or even *inspirational.* Once you have described your current and/or future self, the approaches and actions you take are key factors in building your reputation and establishing credibility early in your career.

Establishing Credibility Early in Your Alt-Ac Career

Credibility is implicit in how you see and describe yourself in work roles or within your discipline. You want people to recognize that you not only know what you are doing but also can contribute to solutions for complex problems or help make advances in the field. Establishing credibility often involves people to know, places to be, and things to do.

People to Know

Start by getting to know the people around you—physically and virtually. At your workplace, take a moment after a meeting to check in with leaders from different units. If you do not know a leader's work well, be prepared by reviewing their bio or unit's website. Mention a common research interest or comment on a new project their team has launched. Beyond your workplace, send an e-mail to people whose research you admire or take a minute to speak with presenters after a conference session. Ask how the ideas they have shared might apply to your work. This allows them to learn about you as well.

We also recommend that you collaborate with veterans on projects or publications. Associating yourself with well-known practitioners provides potential connections to other seasoned professionals, as well as visibility you may not be able to gain on your own. At your workplace, join projects that span the campus or institution, especially those aligned with the mission or strategic plan. You could also propose a research or an assessment project that would involve and benefit multiple institutions.

Places to Be

The places to be to establish credibility may be physical, virtual, or both. For example, provide feedback or information on an electronic mailing list or a discussion forum. Participate in online events, such as webinars, or better yet, facilitate them. At your workplace, you may be in discussion groups for committee work.

Beyond your physical workplace, you may belong to e-mail, discussion, or LinkedIn groups associated with your field or your job role. When you answer others' questions, your peers will come to recognize you as knowledgeable and willing to help others. You can also attend regional meetings or meet-ups for people in your field or for people who play similar roles to your own.

Things to Do

Staying current and keeping your skills up-to-date can happen through activities such as teaching as an adjunct, conducting your own research, coaching students, or doing other tasks that help you hone and grow different skills and abilities. Volunteering to support important initiatives can also help you learn and develop in new areas. At your workplace, start by volunteering to represent your unit in support of a larger project.

Beyond your workplace, volunteering might involve reviewing conference proposals or participating on a conference planning committee. Keep in mind that you will want to appropriately balance your work with outside activities that might enhance your reputation or increase your skills. For example, you may want to seek permission from a boss or supervisor before taking on a time-intensive task such as organizing a conference within your field.

If you want to start publishing as early as possible but do not have a research topic or population, another idea might be to write a meta-analysis that pulls together literature about an emerging topic in your field. In fields such as medicine, meta-analyses are cited more than any other study design (Patsopoulos, Analatos, & Ioannidis, 2005) and can be a great way to help you become a recognized name within your field.

Strategies for Self-Promotion

As you start engaging in activities to establish credibility, you might feel that suggesting things like joint research projects could lead to unflattering descriptors, like *overeager* or *overly ambitious*. You will need to gauge for yourself how receptive people might be to collaboration. (We encourage you to start with activities that don't require asking to insert yourself into someone else's work.)

However, building your reputation, or your professional and personal brand, does involve a certain amount of self-promotion (again, see chapter 27 for more about your personal brand). Many of the activities we listed previously are examples of how to connect with others, build relationships, and promote yourself as trustworthy without seeming pushy. For example, if you answer someone's question in a discussion forum or on an electronic mailing list, you are promoting yourself but through generously sharing your knowledge.

Next Steps

It's time for you to start establishing your reputation. Take a moment to craft a schedule or create a plan that incorporates some of the ideas from this chapter or some of your own. For example, subscribe to a work-related electronic mailing list, discipline-based discussion forum, or LinkedIn group and check it every day for two weeks. Start by answering one or two questions per week. If you do not know the answer yourself, commit to finding the answer by doing some web-based research.

In the next three to six months, find and prepare to participate in a virtual event, such as a webinar, or a live event, such as a meet-up or regional conference. Take the time to research the topic(s) in advance and review the work by the presenter(s). This way you'll be ready to share helpful information when it's time to interact with your peers and colleagues.

19

HAVING EFFECTIVE CONVERSATIONS

In this chapter, you will identify (a) specific goals and potential participants for conversations to have when starting in a new field and (b) strategies for engaging people in those conversations.

Whom to Engage in Effective Conversations and Why

There is only so much web-based research you can do on your own as you attempt to grow in your alt-ac career. At some point, you will want to talk to someone in your field who can answer your questions, who can provide alt-ac career advice, who holds an alt-ac position you want to fill some day, and/or who may even help you get a better job at a different organization. If you are not sure if you know anyone (yet) who falls into one or more of those categories, that's okay. We'll help you find them! These conversations are akin to informational interviews but have a stronger emphasis on being a two-way conversation. You still want to gain knowledge, but you also want to grow the strength and size of your network.

Start With Your Own Network

Before taking on the role as CEO for ASK Educational Games, Ruth Nemire was the senior vice president of the American Association of Colleges of Pharmacy. She encourages people developing alt-ac careers to hold on to connections and mentors. "You don't know where people are going in their own careers and when your paths will cross again." She credits her own connections and mentors with her professional growth— "They're how I've been able to stretch and fly . . . and get opportunities" (R. Nemire, personal communication, February 1, 2018). For example, Nemire is currently publishing standards with someone she met at a study meeting at a past job in Texas. She stayed in touch with him, and he reached out with a collaboration opportunity for which he thought she would be a perfect fit. Even if you do not believe your current and former classmates and colleagues can help you, reach out to them to let them know you are considering an alt-ac position or career. They may have valuable information or, better yet, a job lead.

After exhausting connections involving people you know directly, move to *second-degree connections*; that is, people you can access through your direct connections. When you review the "My Network" list in LinkedIn, click the "See All" link under "Your Connections." When your connections appear, select "Search with Filters" and choose "2nd" from the degrees of connection filter. Then review the resulting profiles to identify people who have positions you may want in one to three years. If you do not use LinkedIn, connect with a current or former adviser or the alumni association from the school where you are earning or earned your graduate degree. Describe the type of person with whom you want to connect and ask if that person would be willing to make a virtual introduction.

If none of these options will work, then consider contacting people at an organization where you'd like to work someday in a leadership role or to move up by moving on (see chapter 21 for more on this). Following the logic in the previous chapter about self-promotion, keep in mind that you are "selling" yourself. After all, you want to give them a reason to open your e-mail and reply. The magazine *Fast Company* studied that very phenomenon. They sent 1,000 *cold e-mails*—that is, they did not know the person they were contacting—to business leaders at the highest levels. While the response rate was very low, two-thirds of the executives opened e-mails with the simple subject line "Quick Question" (Snow, 2014, para. 15). The article also went into detail about increasing chances for a response by making your message "extremely personalized," based on relevant research (which we'll cover later in this chapter), and using "social proof" (Snow, 2014, para. 22) such as seeing or meeting that person at a conference, for credibility.

How to Have Effective Conversations

Before you reach out to anyone you have identified as a potential contact, take the time to do some research that will help you make a stronger connection. As we mentioned in the previous chapter, this may mean reviewing each person's LinkedIn profile, bio page on an organization's website, personal or professional website, and even publications. Make notes about any current projects; recent achievements, such as being awarded a grant or publishing a book; and personal interests. Do your best to identify what is most important now. Drawing a connection between your work and a previous interest is a start, but you should show that you understand what motivates that person at the moment.

You should also be prepared to talk about yourself. While the first conversation should focus more on the other person, be ready with an elevator pitch version of who you want to be "when you grow up." If your time gets cut short for some reason, you want each person to leave your conversation with a good understanding about you, your goal(s), and how they can help you. For example, if your goal is to grow into a leadership position in your interviewee's alt-ac specialty area, then they might provide a list of skills that you need to develop and/or connect you with others in the field. You can always fill in details if you have more time or at a future date.

Requesting a Conversation

Regardless of why you request each conversation, from wanting advice to wanting a specific job, frame it as a request for an informational interview (this was also mentioned back in chapter 7, "Learning More About Alt-Ac Fields"). Even if there is an open position available at their workplace that would help you advance your career, avoid the appearance that the job is the real or only reason you want to talk. Mentioning too early that you are seeking a job could relegate you to the résumé pile with all of the other applicants, at a time when network connections make a big difference in hiring decisions. To drive this point home, the LinkedIn Corporate Communications Team (2017) reported that "70 percent of people in 2016 were hired at a company where they had a connection" (para. 1). So, take the time to make each person a new network connection. If someone you know has recommended contacting this person, make a reference to that connection.

Also, do what you can to avoid exchanging too many e-mails. Be as flexible as you can when proposing days and times in your request (for a sample e-mail template, refer back to chapter 7).

Starting a Conversation

Whether you meet in person or virtually (e.g., phone, videoconference), thank each person in advance for taking the time to talk and confirm how much time the person has to speak with you. Chances are good that the person will be busy, meaning that they may be late to your conversation or may have to leave early. Don't be afraid to offer to reschedule, if you don't think you'll have enough time to accomplish the goals you have set. After you have confirmed the time you have, briefly outline your goal(s) as a reminder.

Then it's time to get the other person talking. As his first two questions during any informational interview, Kelly, one of the authors of this book, always asks, "What's your biggest challenge right now?" and "What are you most excited about?" Another way to word these questions is "What (about your work) keeps you up at night?" and "What motivates you to get up in the morning?" These questions allow your interviewees to outline quickly what occupies their thoughts. If you have several conversations with people from the same field, you may identify patterns. Ideally, you can act as a hub, sharing ideas that you have picked up along the way. See Box 19.1 for a list of potential conversation starters.

Managing a Conversation

In each conversation you will have to balance establishing a rapport with reaching your initial goals; for example, getting advice about publishing or identifying career growth opportunities. It's easy for anyone to start a tangent, so you may have to redirect some interviewees back to the goal(s) that you outlined at the beginning. However, if you see the tangent leading somewhere productive, ask follow-up questions that will guide the conversation in that direction. See Box 19.2 for potential ways to redirect a conversation.

Closing an Initial Conversation

Determine in advance if you plan to make an "ask," or a request for help with something specific, during that initial conversation. Many of us have a hard time asking for something for ourselves, so practice your ask in the mirror in advance. Keep an eye on the time to not only be respectful but also ensure you

BOX 19.1.
Sample Conversation Starters

- What's your biggest challenge at work right now? What are you most excited about?
- What (about your work) keeps you up at night? What motivates you to get up in the morning?
- I'm exploring how to advance in my alt-ac career, and your career path interests me. How did you get to your current position?
- Our field has changed so much in the past 5 to 10 years. What are some niche areas that have the most potential to address the challenges you described?
- What three skills have been most valuable to you throughout your career? How did you get those skills?

BOX 19.2.
Sample Conversation Redirects

- That's interesting! What role did that event play in your decision to pursue an alt-ac leadership position?
- She sounds like an amazing colleague. How have you helped each other reach your individual career goals?
- You have mentored quite a few people throughout your career. How would you recommend finding strong mentors in this field?

can make the ask and address any following questions. Thank each person for taking the time to meet and share with you. See Box 19.3 for potential ways to close a conversation.

Continuing a Conversation
Take the time to send a follow-up thank-you note as soon as you can after each conversation. Let each person know how you will use the answers or advice given to you about your career, people in a position, or a specific job opening, if it got that far. Add value by finding and sharing a recent article about the challenge each person mentioned.

Next Steps

As the adage says, "practice makes perfect." Informational interviews are useful at any point in your journey, so identify one person to contact in the next month to request an informational interview. If for no other reason, you can ask the interviewee to describe how a meaningful alt-ac career was built. Then

BOX 19.3.
Sample Conversation Closing Phrases

- I really appreciate the time you have given me today. May I reach out to you with brief questions as I explore careers in your area of expertise?
- Thank you so much for sharing your thoughts about your role and how I might play a similar role in the future. May I buy you a coffee in a month to thank you and to update you on my progress?
- You have provided a lot of valuable information in a short time! Thank you. May I send you a summary of my notes, in case you have any other suggestions about resources for me to check out?

follow the steps outlined in this chapter to prepare for and request your first conversation. Use the remaining steps to make that conversation effective and to follow it with a meaningful note.

PART FIVE

GROWING IN THE ALT-AC SPACE

P art Five is all about working and networking in the alt-ac space. For those interested in consulting work, we share real-world tips about logistics, marketing, networking, and other critical functions. We describe how to work your way up within an organization—or move up by moving on. We show you strategies for writing outside of your initial discipline, finding publication pipelines in new fields, and producing media such as podcasts or blogs. We also discuss how to increase the size and reach of your professional networks through professional organizations and how to get the most out of them.

20

DOING CONSULTING WORK

In this chapter, you will learn how to (a) get started and then (b) stand out in your alt-ac consulting work, whether you are giving speeches, facilitating workshops, or doing full-blown project consulting.

From Giving Talks to Being a Consultant

At some point in your academic career, some of you reading this book may have been approached by colleagues at other colleges and universities who asked a version of the question that started Tobin down his own alt-ac path: "That was great! Do you consult?"

Tobin started consulting before he started consulting. In other words, Tobin's first consulting connections were based on chance encounters. Just after he earned his PhD in 2000, Tobin led the development team creating then-brand-new online courses at a two-year college in Pennsylvania. On the basis of his experiences, he crafted a white paper about "time-critical online course development" (Tobin, 2000) and presented it at a local consortium's conference.

So far, this all matched what he had been taught to do in his humanities graduate studies: do the research, write the article, and present the article (i.e., read it verbatim) at a conference. A colleague who attended the conference asked Tobin if he would present his ideas in a workshop at the colleague's university, asking, "What are your rates for speaking?"

Tobin had no idea how to respond. He took the colleague's card and spent the following afternoon trying to find guidance about how much to charge and how to create contracts for outside consulting—even whether or not he was allowed to accept such an offer, because he was attending the conference as a representative of his own college. Even though Tobin didn't find anything to help him, he he was able to clear the event with his associate vice president ("I'm glad you asked, but what you do on your own time is up to you; take a vacation day"), cobble together a price ($250.00), agree to terms with the university (it had a standard consultant contract), and present his first workshop as an external consultant. This led to another invitation to facilitate a discussion series for a state-wide government agency.

Consulting Is a Many-Sided Thing

The term *consulting* can mean many things. For many alt-ac practitioners, it does not mean joining a consulting firm and working there full-time. Rather, we are talking about paying side gigs: speaking, giving workshops, facilitating short courses, recording webinars—doing contract work of all kinds. Most readers of this book will want to prepare for the occasional consulting contract, and we will show you in this chapter how best to be ready for those conversations. A few of you will want to explore whether your independent work can become a full-time endeavor (see chapter 27 on establishing a personal brand). Whether you want to consult a few times a year or you want to establish your own independent alt-ac business, you will want to address a few common obstacles.

Mind-Set Challenges

Before you start consulting, we recommend that you do a little myth busting to help set yourself up to approach consulting in a purposeful way. Some ideas about our work as scholars get in the way of consulting success. Here are three such myths.

First, "self-promotion is unscholarly." This idea is not as prevalent in graduate programs and department meetings as it once was, but it's definitely still a thing. This thinking goes something like this: Because we are all part of a larger scholarly community, it is crass to place monetary value on what we do, except in a very limited set of circumstances, such as grants, patents, and fellowships. Typically, if we try to earn money outside of these well-established systems, we can be perceived as selling out. We are implicitly encouraged to share our ideas and work freely, for the good of the department, institution, or field of study.

This has led to armies of graduate students and tenure-line faculty members dutifully registering to read their research papers in 15-minute slots at large conferences just to be able to say they have taken an active role in scholarly communication—Tobin did his share of this as a graduate student at MLA conferences over the years. One way to combat this viewpoint is to realize that many funders of scholarly research, such as the National Science Foundation and the Canada Council, explicitly want scholars to consider the broader impacts of their work beyond the academy; fortunately, the idea of commercial or public benefit is starting to find a place in colleges and universities.

The second myth is that "no one will want to hear what I have to say; I'm just starting out." This mind-set leads many academics—even those who are many years into their careers—to view themselves as having to pay their dues in a publish-or-perish culture where journal-article space and conference-presentation slots are limited-access prizes. The feeling that one cannot compete, especially when comparing oneself to more experienced or better resourced colleagues, can lead to thinking that there are a limited number of opportunities out there, and we had better settle for what comes our way. This sort of nascent *imposter syndrome*, in which we downplay our competence because we feel that others are the real experts, is common among people who gain expertise in many fields (see Hermann, 2016).

Third, many of us suffer from some version of someday-my-prince-will-come syndrome, where we follow the dictum that our hard work and determination will one day be noticed by someone who will recognize and reward it. Although this does happen, it can be rare. When a colleague actually approached Tobin early in his career to ask about his speaking rates, he was ill-prepared to respond because the request came as a surprise. The myth of "hoping to be recognized" fails to take into account the tendency of the recognizer to expect the talent (you) to have clear processes already in place for working with others as a consultant.

Logistics (or, How Much Do I Charge?)

Frequently, one of the most challenging parts about consulting is figuring out how to position yourself in terms of what to charge for your services. All of us want to value our work appropriately, yet there are few places where people actually talk about the numbers involved. Some published advice is helpful in understanding what goes into the how-much-to-charge decision, such as Brian Croxall's (2013) article "What's Your Speaking Fee?":

> Consider the fact that although you'll be giving, say, just an hour-long talk that you will have to spend several hours—if not a whole day each way—traveling. In other words, if you recoil at asking for X for that 60-minute talk and Q&A, realize that you'll be spending much more than an hour on the visit and taking time from your other work.
>
> Consider the preparation that you'll have to do for the visit. Will you be leading a workshop that you've done previously? Will it be a brand-new talk, on a subject that you are just exploring? If it's the latter, you will again be putting in a lot more time than simply that one hour.

Consider whether your speaking fee should always be the same or whether it should flex according to the group or institution inviting you. A group of grad students asking you to come to speak will probably have much different resources than the chair of a department at Princeton. Likewise, small state schools or consortia might not be as flush as R1 universities.

Consider asking colleagues or friends about what they charge for speaking fees. Your discipline might have common practices that you are not aware of.

However, even Croxall does not say how much he actually charges. Most advice in this realm is less than useful, such as the blanket "don't charge less than a thousand dollars" that we saw posted recently in the comments section of an especially exasperating blog posting.

Here is one back-of-the-envelope way to set your speaking and consulting rate. Bring to mind the salary that people in your field typically earn at your level of experience. For mid-career humanities practitioners, for example, this number might be $75,000.00 a year. Of course, this will be different depending on your field, your level of experience, and your geographic location, but start with a number that fits your circumstances. Now, divide that by 52 to obtain a weekly rate (in our example, $1,442.31) and then again by 40 to arrive at an hourly rate ($36.06). Now, start building. Tally up the amount of time you will spend in communication, development, travel, and delivery for a client. For example, for a 90-minute invited workshop, the preparation will involve several actions that add up to a significant amount of time, including

- communicating via e-mail, phone calls, video calls, and other methods (5 hours);
- conducting research about the institution, website reading, and learning directly from colleagues about their department or program (10 hours);
- drafting the presentation, handouts, worksheets, rating form, white paper, and takeaways for participants (20 hours);
- booking hotel, airfare, and rental car, along with other logistical planning with the client about the day of the event (5 hours);
- traveling, staying overnight, facilitating the event itself, and traveling back home (35 hours); and
- collating post-event ratings, video editing, and following up with the client for testimonials and billing (5 hours).

Every consultation is an iceberg, with the actual visible event supported by a great, invisible amount of work. In our example, the 90-minute workshop is only a tiny part of the 80 total hours of time invested—two full work weeks of effort. Multiply the 80 hours by the calculated hourly rate of $36.06, and we arrive at $2,884.80. Note that this is what you would charge for your effort alone and does not include separate payment for things like hotel and airfare costs.

Whether you choose to round up or down, the hourly rate formula works surprisingly well at defining at least a starting point for setting your base fees. Depending on the salary that you'd like to earn, crafting an estimate for the total effort involved helps you to see how much you should value your work in a rough-numbers way. There is also something to be said for rounding up or even adding 10% to 15% to your newly calculated rate to cover things such as self-employment taxes and insurance, if you wish to consult full-time. Some also say that more expensive speakers are often perceived—rightly or wrongly—as being more desirable. While we don't go so far as to endorse this last strategy for everyone, as you create your materials to support your efforts, it helps to start from a slightly higher price point and adjust down or up based on the clients whom you attract.

The Myth of "Exposure"

As you begin creating an identity as a speaker or professional facilitator, beware the voices telling you to lower your rates. You may hear advice to speak or work for free or for a very low fee, simply to get an endorsement or to say that you presented at Prestigious Institution X or Y. We recommend you be cautious with this advice. If people at a college or university are interested in having you speak or work with their faculty and staff, either they will pay your fee or they will say it is out of their budget. Each of the authors of this book has worked with clients to negotiate different fees from time to time, but we also say no to lowball offers. Never work just for the exposure.

Colleagues will also tell you that you should charge less for a presentation that you have already developed, because it is already "in the can." Even experienced speakers and consultants sometimes fall into a routine where they share the same presentation, the same way, regardless of the audience. For huge-name speakers who speak to conferences of thousands of people, having a standard speech or approach is an efficient operating method. You, too, should have a standard version of the speeches, workshops, and interactions that you typically do. However, working with colleges and universities, especially when audiences will be in the tens or hundreds of people, presents an opportunity to stand out from the crowd of speakers and consultants whom they invite to campus.

We argue that any time that you save on content preparation by giving an existing version of a presentation should get reinvested into learning more about your client's campus and climate. We have seen many people speak cold at conferences and faculty in-service days, and such speakers often misread the audience or offer ideas that are already in common use at the host institution. Always do your homework when you are able to do so (this is part of what clients are paying for, by the way).

One way to do your homework is by talking with faculty members and staff at your host institution ahead of time about their college's or university's culture and unique characteristics. The real power behind this approach is not learning details about your host's politics and campus processes (valuable though that is) but rather that it will set you apart if you take the time to really listen to clients. Just the act of saying "I want to know more about what is important to you," and then acting on what you hear, sets you apart from the majority of other speakers and consultants. We can't tell you how often we hear people who have invited us to their campuses say, "No one has ever asked us about our goals and culture before coming to speak with us." If you want to take your consulting and speaking to the next level, be a listener.

Marketing Your Services

A paradox in starting your consulting efforts is that although you will need content to support your services, you are unlikely to know what to put into your gigs until after you have done a few of them. This chicken-and-egg problem can be confusing, unless you do the thought exercises that we outlined in the preceding sections. To get the word out about what you do, you will need to create some specific materials and then share them in various ways. Many consultants have a fee schedule, or speaker's brochure, where they list the general topics about which they often speak and consult (e.g., see Tobin, 2018). Having a website of your own that focuses on the work you do (e.g., see drkatielinder.com and thomasjtobin.com) is a first step to getting the word out about what you do.

To really get the word out, though, you have to be an active participant in the conversations where people discuss the problems and issues that you can address. When you present at professional conferences in your area, ask ahead of time if it's all right to include one thank-you slide at the end of your presentation that lists your topics of expertise. Then, out loud, say, "I really enjoyed working with all of you on this topic. I speak and consult in this area, and if you'd like to continue the conversation, come see me after the session or grab one of my business cards."

In the same way, post your ideas to online discussion groups; write brief issue pieces for magazines, journals, and blogs in your field; and send opinion pieces to your local newspapers and scholarly organizations' newsletters. Remember that it's all right to position yourself as an expert facilitator and ask that people who are interested in working with you to contact you.

Getting There

One final practical note: How do speakers handle travel logistics such as booking flights, arranging hotel stays, and paying for meals and other incidental costs during a speaking consultation? The answer to this question is a definite "it depends." Instead of asking your clients how they prefer to handle such arrangements, craft a section of your website or speaking brochure that deals with logistics. Some colleges and universities must make travel and hotel bookings themselves or through their travel agencies; work with them closely to ensure that you end up in a decent place and on flights that don't make you get up at 3:00 a.m. or sit in a connecting airport for four hours (believe us, this happens a lot).

Even better, if you are able to make such bookings yourself and then ask for reimbursement from the client, you can have a modicum of control over how you travel and where you stay, which allows you to rack up frequent-flier miles and preferred-guest points. In any case, prepare a help-me-travel, single-page file that includes a copy of your passport or driver's license, your known traveler number with the Transportation Safety Administration (trust us, you'll want to get one), and your frequent-flier and guest numbers at various airlines, hotels, and car rental companies.

Next Steps

As you focus on how to create content and processes that will jump-start your speaking or consulting work, if you remember nothing else, remember to do your homework. Figure out what you can say that will help others in your field. Even if you aren't the world's leading expert in your topic area, perhaps position yourself as an affordable alternative to the big-name experts and focus on the results and practical use-them-tomorrow takeaways that you can share with clients.

Once you start creating a website and speaking brochure, seek out the people who are speaking and consulting in your field and talk with them about how they got started; how they determined their own balance of speaking and other work; and, confidentially, how they determined how much they charge clients. We have found that colleagues who consult are usually pretty open and welcoming to newer speakers, especially because professional speaking is very much a team sport: Connections in the field recommend one another to clients, who always ask, "Who should we bring to campus next?"

If you want to do a deeper dive into speaking and consulting, we recommend reading a combination of academic and general resources:

- R. M. Bodenheimer (2017), "The Plight of the Independent Scholar"
- J. Carter (2013), *The Message of You: Turn Your Life Story Into a Money-Making Speaking Career*
- D. Clark (2015), *Stand Out: How to Find Your Breakthrough Idea and Build a Following Around It*
- P. Shankman (2015), *Zombie Loyalists: Using Great Service to Create Rabid Fans*
- C. Simon (2016), *Impossible to Ignore: Creating Memorable Content to Influence Decisions*
- A. W. Strouse (2017), "Transcending the Job Market"
- J. Warner (2017), "My After-Academia Role Models"

A number of these are our go-to resources for practical tips, and we know that these books and articles will reward further exploration.

Remember the story of Tobin's very first speaking engagement that opened this chapter? He has now been speaking and consulting professionally for many years. Along the way, he has worked with—and booked for his university's own events—colleagues whose consulting ranged from mediocre to outstanding. What set the best speakers apart from the rest? They listened.

21

WORKING UP INTERNALLY OR MOVING UP BY MOVING ON

In this chapter, you will (a) consider the various career stages of different alt-ac positions in colleges, universities, and academic-adjacent institutions—and their similarities to and differences from faculty career stages—and (b) learn the benefits and challenges of advancing with one employer versus transitioning to a new institution.

The Alt-Ac Road Map Has Some Blank Spaces

In our graduate school training, most of us get a good sense of what it will take to move through the process of becoming faculty members. We teach, attend conferences, publish our research, and serve our institutions and our fields, knowing that all of these activities will help us move along a career path with milestones that are fairly well marked for us. For example, the typical faculty path at U.S. and Canadian institutions follows a ranking hierarchy with specific requirements for moving from one to the next.

Instructors are hired on an as-needed basis to teach courses or supervise lab sessions. Assistant professors are entry-level, full-time faculty members who are on the tenure track, usually with teaching, research, publication, and service expectations. Associate professors have earned tenure and can focus their efforts on narrower service commitments to their departments or fields. Full professors are recognized for their prominence in and contributions to their institutions and fields of study. Although there are increasingly fewer tenure-line positions available at colleges and universities these days (Griffey, 2017), many graduate programs train their students how to be and do academic culture within this tenure-track model.

Contrast this model to alt-ac positions within colleges and universities. While few graduate programs prepare their students for such careers, this is hardly their fault, because there is no standard model for alt-ac career paths. Some alt-ac professionals have proposed general models, but they often depend on going through training for faculty positions and then pivoting to an alt-ac option (e.g., Kim, 2016). Although this is a common experience among alt-ac professionals early in our careers, general models also present a challenge because of the range of entry points to alt-ac roles.

Unlike in the faculty model, many alt-ac positions in colleges and universities are created to fill specific administrative needs, both in traditional curriculum-support roles (e.g., teaching, tutoring, multimedia, and instructional-design centers) and in outreach areas of the institution (e.g., university presses, continuing education centers, alumni outreach, and marketing and/or communications). The alt-ac space is so varied, in fact, that there are a number of online resources dedicated to helping PhDs narrow their alt-ac job searches. ImaginePhD, for instance, groups alt-ac careers into a number of different categories; here are a few from its list:

- Advocacy
- Communications, public relations, and marketing
- Consulting
- Development
- Higher education administration
- Human services
- Organizational management
- Research and analysis
- Training
- Translation and interpretation
- Writing, publishing, and editing (Graduate Career Consortium, 2018)

We will cover writing and publishing in chapter 22 and joining professional organizations in chapter 23. Now, we want to focus on how to plan an alt-ac career within higher education and how to know when to create a path within your institution or when to move to a new institution to pursue your alt-ac career trajectory.

Beth Seltzer is an academic technology specialist at Stanford University, and she is an excellent example of someone who followed the alt-ac career path without much early-career guidance but who found a good path with help from the alt-ac field. Seltzer earned a PhD in Victorian literature, then worked in the administrations at Temple University, the University of Pennsylvania, Bryn Mawr College, and now Stanford. As a doctoral student, she obtained a slot in the first cohort of fellows for MLA's Connected Academics Proseminar, which provided the type of alt-ac career guidance and support that traditional humanities programs did not.

Seltzer recently published a study of MLA job postings showing that while alt-ac skills are in demand, most PhD programs "don't teach them explicitly" (quoted in Jaschik, 2018). After Seltzer published an article on alt-ac job candidates for *Connected Academics* (Seltzer, 2016), we reached out to her to hear more of her story:

> I was at Temple for my graduate education. I knew, going in, that I really didn't want to be a long-term adjunct. I had the chance to see what that lifestyle entails, and I didn't want it to be mine. So I started looking around pretty early. Over the summer, I was working on a digital scholarship project—the Early Novels Database Project, which involves a couple of colleges and universities. I was going to the Penn library every day, and I made some contacts there who helped me get a post-doc at Penn in the library. I think there are, increasingly, post-doc, transitional positions for PhDs. I learned a ton of different skills that were useful for working in libraries. But, because it was a post-doc, it was a term position, so, as I was doing that, I was applying for other jobs.
>
> I think administration—being able to organize and lead people and projects—is one of the top, broadly applicable skills for PhDs. I felt like it was something that we really didn't talk about in grad school, but there were also plenty of opportunities to develop this skill in grad school. One of the TA-ships I had was helping to run the First Year Writing program as a Composition Assistant. It was super useful, lots of great experience, and a good alternative to traditional teaching TA-ships, but teaching TA-ships were far more common. I have a friend who was actually able to talk herself into a TA-ship working with the dean's office at the grad school, so she was gaining a whole other skill set while still doing TA-like work for the university. I would say administration is a transferable skill that also showed up in my research as being especially useful for academic jobs. (B. Seltzer, personal communication, January 23, 2018)

Seltzer's identification of her key nonfaculty skills in administration helped her apply for many different kinds of positions:

> My last year on the job market, I was looking for jobs that had four different job titles: assistant-professor jobs, ed tech, librarian, and digital-scholarship specialist positions. . . . I was at least the second choice or got a job offer in all four of those fields, which is crazy! It was a lot. (B. Seltzer, personal communication, January 23, 2018)

Seltzer was trying out different jobs, fields, and areas of expertise based on her own experiences and her examination of what employers were asking for. This brings up a question: Is there a more systematic way to prepare for alt-ac jobs? Knowing something about alt-ac career paths helps.

Is There an Alt-Ac Career Ladder?

Despite the variety among alt-ac jobs, for those of us who want to establish alt-ac career paths within higher education, there are career stages common to most alt-ac positions, and they are roughly analogous to the faculty career path through instructor and assistant, associate, and full professorships. No matter what types of alt-ac positions you are interested in, if you want to stay within a college or university, expect to move "up the ladder" according to the following progression. Note the key words that you will likely find in job titles and descriptions as well.

- Entry-level positions: In both student-support and faculty-support areas, entry-level positions target those who do not yet have terminal degrees in their fields or people without advanced degrees in the service area. These positions are the most focused on operational-level tasks and are unlikely to have supervisory or project responsibilities. Analogous to the instructor level in the tenure-track model, these positions can be contract-based or full-time roles. Look for job titles such as assistant, designer, specialist, and technician.
- Associate-level positions: Analogous to the assistant-professor level in the tenure-track hierarchy (and not the associate-professor level), associate-level alt-ac positions are primarily operations based but with the added component of significant self-directed work or project responsibility. These positions typically require an advanced degree in the alt-ac area, in a subject field, or both. The most common job title is associate (e.g., "research associate"); look also for analyst, consultant, and administrator titles.
- Coordinators: Coordinator positions nearly always include a significant supervisory role, project management responsibilities, and a mix of operational and strategic duties. Similar to associate professors in the tenure-track model, coordinators have usually put in the work of five or more years in the alt-ac field, with a demonstrated record of projects, initiatives, grants, and results to show for it. In addition to the job title of coordinator, look for manager and assistant director positions as well.

- Directors: At the top of the alt-ac hierarchy are director-level positions. In faculty-services and student-services areas, directors are typically responsible for the performance of entire departments or campus units, such as the registrar, tutoring center, or teaching and learning center. Their duties are largely strategic and supervisory, including budgeting, staffing, and strategic planning. Most director-level alt-ac positions require some years of experience in the field, with progressively greater responsibility at each career stage. Directors are similar to full professors in the tenure-track hierarchy, especially because this is as high in the model as one can get before one has to move into campus leadership (e.g., to a chair, dean, or vice president role) to advance one's career. This level of position is almost always denoted with the words director, managing director, or executive director.

The majority of alt-ac positions within colleges and universities lead only as far as the director level. Traditionally, the senior leadership roles in higher education are closed, or at least very challenging to get, for those of us who come up through the alt-ac route. Department chairpersons and deans are most often selected from among the ranks of the faculty (Caldwell, 2014), even though the core skills for most upper-level administrators—such as risk assessment, project management, and systemic visioning—seem to be found less often among faculty members and more often among those in alt-ac roles in colleges and universities (Butin, 2016).

This unofficial ceiling for the alt-ac career path within colleges and universities brings up an important question for all of us in the alt-ac job space: Is it better to remain with one institution and work one's way up through the various ranks of alt-ac jobs, or is it better to develop one's skills in one institution and then move to another college or university to move "up and out" to a new role? This question is especially pertinent to ask when one notes that the tenure-track model asks faculty members to produce tangible and quantifiable products to show their skills: articles, books, presentations, student ratings, and so on (Kim, 2017). However, alt-ac staff members and administrators are seldom asked to collect similar evidence of skills or accumulated expertise. We might have a hard time standardizing what to ask for, because of the diversity of alt-ac positions, even if we wanted to create some common categories. So what's an alt-ac professional to do?

Deciding Your Next Career Moves

There are pros and cons to working within one academic institution versus moving among several colleges and universities as an alt-ac career strategy.

From a scientific point of view, the goal that you want to achieve is called *equifinality* (Jiménez & Escalante, 2017): the state, in open systems such as higher education, of having multiple paths that lead to the same outcome—in this case, a stable and rewarding alt-ac career.

A word of caution: The following analysis purposely ignores many big factors that go into any decision about whether to remain in one institution or find new positions elsewhere, such as socioeconomic, gender, subject field, and family commitment factors (e.g., Heyl & Damron, 2014). By acknowledging that all of these factors will vary significantly, we are modeling our ideas on open systems theory—in short, this advice is based on knowing what you can and cannot control in your career planning.

The Case for Remaining With One Institution for a Long Time

The largest advantage of remaining in one college or university for the majority of your alt-ac career is that you get to show your skills in concrete ways that people remember, allowing you to build and advance your career in a format that you have a greater hand in shaping as a "stayer."

The flip side of being a stayer can be a drawback, however, where the very familiarity that your colleagues have with you leads them to see you only in terms of your immediate and day-to-day interactions with them rather than in terms of your overall accomplishments and value to the institution—a sort of "oh, it's no one special, just our colleague" syndrome.

For example, we spoke with Valerie Kisiel, who cofounded Innovative Educators, about why she decided to make the ultimate alt-ac move and start her own company:

> We started—gosh, it's been 14 years, now. There were three of us who started it: myself, Erin Hoag, and Pam Ranallo, and we all worked at a community college in Colorado in different capacities. I was in advising and online student services. Erin was a dean, and Pam was a faculty member.
>
> I had attended a conference from one of our current competitors and felt like it was lacking, and I could tell they really didn't have a higher-ed background. Erin and I had run some conferences together at Front Range Community College. I said, "I think there's something here; I think we could do it better than they're doing it and be less expensive." They were charging really high prices. We started brainstorming and decided, let's just do it. We started with the webinars first. Our first webinar was in June . . . and then by November, it really started picking up. I said, "You know what? I'll quit." I continued to work part-time at Front Range but then worked full-time for the company.

We were all in different places in our careers. Erin and Pam are older and had invested more years in their retirement plans on campus. Luckily, I was at a point in my career where I was okay giving it up or taking the risk. It was scary, but I think what was scarier for me was knowing exactly where I would be in 10 years. Envisioning my growth at Front Range wasn't very exciting to me. Staying was probably scarier than leaving, from an emotional standpoint. (V. Kisiel, personal communication, January 29, 2018)

Moving Up by Moving On

If staying with one institution allows you the relative security of knowing what the career path looks like (and possibly having a hand in shaping it), it can also lead to burnout or a truncated career path (Wöhrer, 2014, pp. 471–473). As we saw from Seltzer's story, moving from institution to institution is becoming a norm in the alt-ac world, and it is increasingly rare for hiring managers even to expect to find candidates who will remain with the college or university for their entire careers:

> [Although] concerns about looking like a job-hopper or even a failure weighed on some people's minds, . . . the workplace is radically different now than it was 15 or 20 years ago. Keeping your career moving forward is paramount, and in a lot of cases, it's counterproductive to stay in one place. Time on the job, "experience," etc., don't count as much as having the right skill set. (Vailiancourt, 2013, p. 53)

While we do not go so far as to recommend Deepak Malhotra's advice to "quit early, quit often" (Malhotra, 2012), crafting a career among many institutions carries significant benefits of its own. For example, as we demonstrate throughout this book, alt-ac careers are well suited to variety and complexity, with a main line of work as an anchor to many side gigs like speaking, consulting, and publishing. Planning for an alt-ac career that purposely moves among different institutions enhances your sense of broadening your experiences and meeting new challenges regularly. In terms of enhancing your attractiveness to the next college or university who might hire you, planning to get experience in a variety of settings (e.g., two year, four year, and university; public and private; rural and urban) can make you a more well-rounded candidate and colleague. We've found that especially early in a career, you can benefit from some institution hopping every two or three years. Val Kisiel also spoke to us about the decision-making process for some of her colleagues:

Erin and Pam didn't want to leave [their work at the community college], and Pam has since left our company, just last year, because she had made the decision that she wants to focus on teaching and doesn't really want to own a business. Erin left the [community college] system office [in 2014] and started working for us full-time. We all left the college at different times: It was definitely challenging, at times. (V. Kisiel, personal communication, January 29, 2018)

We will talk more in chapters 28 and 29 about moving between alt-ac and faculty roles; the examples we share here can help you engage in the thought process for deciding where you want to go next.

Next Steps

If your goal is to forge an alt-ac career inside higher education, knowing whether you plan to claim your career ladder in one place or among many institutions will help you craft and strengthen relationships that can further your goals. A first step, once you have made your choice, is to engage with the people who can validate and support your career. If you are a "stayer," volunteer for campus-wide committees or projects that get you in touch with people whom you would not ordinarily interact. Start to learn the interpersonal, political, social, and infrastructure systems at your institution.

If you are a "goer," spend a lot of your energy in professional groups in your field; get to know the people at other institutions who do what you do. Collaborate with them on articles, conference presentations, and data-gathering projects that benefit higher education generally. It's always great to walk into an interview and say, "I was part of the team that made X easier for you."

The silver lining to all of this advice is, paradoxically, not to take it as written in stone. Once you choose to stay with your institution, that does not mean that you cannot go for an opportunity at another college or university that would be a better fit or help you advance your work or life goals. Events can change in ways that cause us to reconsider our original plans. Knowing how to pivot effectively and how to navigate the stages of alt-ac careers provides you with a set of goals that can flex with you as your career advances. By keeping your options open and considering different types of positions, you can provide needed flexibility for moving within or among institutions when life or job circumstances change. Later, we will end this book with a story about a colleague, Todd Zakrajsek, who moved through both types of situations successfully. His story is in the conclusion. But first, let's explore the writing and publishing opportunities for alt-ac professionals.

22

WRITING AND PUBLISHING

In this chapter, you will (a) learn about the various publication opportunities for alt-ac professionals and (b) explore how publishing can help with career progression.

Publish or Perish . . . or Maybe Not

We alt-ac professionals have a built-in advantage when it comes to taking part in the larger conversation around our professional fields: Most of us are in jobs where we have practical goals. How many times have you read a blog, journal article, or book that offered advice on how to simplify complex ideas, perform tasks more smoothly, or interact with colleagues more productively? (We hope that this book does all of these things, by the way.)

Now, think about your own experiences. Think back to the last time you explained a technique or thought through an issue in conversation with a friend, student, or coworker. If your audience benefited from that inter-action, chances are others would as well. You can use all the skills that you have gained throughout not only your academic training but also your alt-ac career to contribute to a successful writing and publishing effort.

We should say that while two fulfilling alt-ac paths are working full-time in the publishing industry and working as a writer for a company or insti-tution, this chapter is about how to incorporate writing and publishing in other types of alt-ac positions.

Because publication is not a job requirement in many alt-ac roles, there is seldom the publish-or-perish pressure for alt-ac professionals that our col-leagues in tenure-track faculty positions might feel. For example, many alt-acs may not need to write journal articles and books to get to the next stage of their careers. However, we think that being part of the alt-ac community means sharing your voice, experiences, and wisdom with others, and writing is a powerful way to do that.

This chapter will show you how to start small and expand your writing and publishing efforts. We will show you what publishers look for in authors and how to make your publishing serve your other alt-ac efforts, such as speaking, consulting, and day-job work. Establishing a publication record can strengthen your reputation, network, and skill set, all things that help you advance along the alt-ac career path that we talked about in chapter 21.

Types of Alt-Ac Writing

There are many different kinds of writing that you can share with broader audiences. Some of these include writing such as experience sharing, process analysis, and strategic thinking. Other forms of writing may fit into what is considered more typical for academic publishing, such as sharing results from a study or research project. Although this is neither an exhaustive list nor exclusive to alt-ac professionals, these writing forms are a useful place to start thinking about how and where you want to share your alt-ac ideas.

Experience Sharing

Experience sharing is the kind of writing in which you say, "Here is what happened to me" or "This is how I thought this situation through." Contrary to what you may have been trained to think about professional writing, there is little need here for scholarly citation or an overly formal tone, although if you do refer to other sources, at least insert hyperlinks in the text. If you have undergone an experience that relates to your career or the practice of your job—and it has helped you gain some insight—write it up. Avoid an easy mistake and do not send these types of pieces to the flagship journals in your field. One step up from posting a long entry on your own personal blog is to send one of your experiential writing pieces to a daily or weekly publication for people in your field (e.g., *The Chronicle of Higher Education*, *Inside Higher Ed*, *Campus Technology*, a discipline-based association's blog, etc.). Make sure that you have a central question to ask of readers or a key takeaway that readers can try out for themselves.

Process Analysis

Process analysis is where alt-ac writing really shines. If you have figured out a better, smoother, different, easier way to do some task or process, write it up. Even if you have an idea for how a task could be strengthened, take a few minutes to write about it. Do not be afraid to ask your readers for help in carrying out ideas and experiments, either. Pitch your tone and scholarly rigor in the midpoint through citing sources using a formal system and adopting the stance of an informed practitioner. The aim is to be a bit less off-the-cuff than in experiential writing but not so formal as to produce a research paper like you would have done as a graduate student. These sorts of written pieces are usually aimed at journals and other outlets that have peer-review processes.

Writing About Strategies

Strategic writing (or a "think piece") is typically aimed at wide audiences, and you will have your best luck getting this type of submission published in newsletters and magazines hosted by professional organizations (e.g., *EDUCAUSE Review* or *Journal of the American Chemical Society*). Base your writing on your understanding of the field as it is today, talk with a number of colleagues and predict where key trends will go, or write about what your organization is doing to respond to new developments in the field. Do not overlook traditional print media here either. Informed letters to the editor of major newspapers are a good way to practice on a small scale with ideas that you wish to expand later into articles or books.

Sharing Results

This form of writing may be the most familiar to you, no matter what your experience level in academia, because it is the most common type of writing that we often *read* as graduate students. Peer-reviewed articles, book chapters, monographs, and other publications that share results from studies in a range of fields are the coin of the realm in traditional academia. Many alt-acs continue to publish in traditional ways, even when this is not required for a current alt-ac role, because they genuinely enjoy it. Others want to stay engaged with their field or discipline. Still others hope to eventually leverage their more traditional publication record into a faculty role. There are many reasons alt-acs keep their hand in traditional publishing throughout their career, even if juggling research "on the side" can be a bit of a challenge.

Old School Versus New School

Professional communication, learning, and development today are very different from how things were even 10 years ago. Shehata, Ellis, and Foster (2017) recently published findings about how we go about interacting, seeking information, collaborating, and publishing information for our professional development. They identified three groups: orthodox, moderate, and heterodox:

(1) Orthodox . . . traditional formal scholarly communication practices are the strongly preferred approach to research.
(2) Moderate . . . adhere to traditional scholarly communication practices. Modern communication methods are used when it is necessary, though [they are] not used in activities such [as] scholarly publishing or as a resource of information.
(3) Heterodox . . . use informal and formal scholarly communication in all scholarly communication stages . . . [and] are heavily dependent on the social web to conduct their research. (p. 830)

Here are some alt-ac examples of each type of communication. Research institute scholars share their findings via orthodox methods and channels: traditional reports and journal articles. Teaching and learning center staff typically work in moderate communication models: the scholarship of teaching and learning (SoTL) is more formal, and communications to faculty colleagues are placed into less formal channels. Speakers and consultants are highly heterodox in their communications: They are at their best when they are playing the role of radical simplifiers; think of scholars like the astronomer Neil deGrasse Tyson who speak to popular audiences.

Because of this fragmentation of ways in which we conduct the overall conversations within and about our fields, there are a number of avenues for sharing your writing with colleagues, from informal methods (e.g., blogging and taking part in wikis, electronic mailing lists, and old-fashioned e-mail) to more rigorous practices (e.g., submitting articles to magazines and journals). One question to ask yourself as you consider an alt-ac pathway is to what degree would you like to publish and in what formats?

What Do Publishers Want?

The authors of this book have published in a number of different formats and styles on wide-ranging topics. Editors and publishers at all levels are interested in work that matches their aim, scope, and audience. Examining the processes and practices in which we engage as we go about our work is always a good angle. As alt-ac professionals, all of us have key insights to share with our colleagues. There are many productive places to look for publication opportunities.

Especially if you are starting out in your alt-ac career, we advocate writing your own blog for magazine-style publications, for professional-development companies, and for submitting to journals in your field. As an alt-ac professional, you should be publishing not because you feel that you must or because it will help you check a box on a job application but

because being part of a larger conversation in the field brings you immediate or long-term benefits. Have a reason to publish, and your path will
likely be smoother right from the start.

Next Steps

As you think about your own goals for writing as an alt-ac, start reading and
experiencing the types of publications in which you might like to publish
your own material. Once you get a feel for the publication, review its website
for submission guidelines. Get a sense of the topics, tone, length, and level of
rigor expected in a given publication. For example, *Inside Higher Ed* is always
looking for brief experiential pieces about the condition of specific alt-ac
populations; *eLearn Magazine* wants longer format process analysis pieces
based on actual practices without being so rigorous as to be too dense for a
general readership; and the *Journal of Interactive Online Learning* is looking
for highly rigorous, research-based submissions. Many organizations list and
describe the types of papers they accept for their journals. For instance, visit
https://publications.agu.org/author-resource-center/paper-types to see what
the American Geophysical Union accepts.

Once you know what your target publications want, e-mail or call the
editors and pitch an idea to see if it fits with their needs; often, editors can
help you figure out not only whether your idea is right for their publication but also when it should come out so that it will chime with other
relevant work from others. Do not get discouraged if you encounter "no,
thank you," either: The publish-or-perish culture among our tenure-track
colleagues has made editors a cautious bunch these days.

Another important step can be to network and form connections with
other alt-ac writers. As you build your alt-ac communities, see who else is
publishing and where they are placing their work. Consider forming an
alt-ac writing group for additional support and accountability.

Last, to ensure that your writing muscles stay warm, we recommend
blogging. Whether you have your own professional website and self-
hosted blog or you choose to publish on a group blogging platform such
as Medium, blog writing is a great way to reflect on your own experiences
and share what you are learning with others.

23

JOINING AND PARTICIPATING IN PROFESSIONAL ORGANIZATIONS

In this chapter, you will find (a) examples of professional organizations for alt-ac professionals inside and outside of higher education settings and (b) tips on how to become an active networker through phone calls, social media, and in-person connections.

Alt-Ac Collaborations

Just as faculty members have their own disciplinary advocacy groups and provosts have their own professional organization, those of us in the alt-ac space can take advantage of a number of professional groups in our various fields. One of the upsides to alt-ac practice is that even though our institutions are, at least on paper, competitors to one another, alt-ac professionals from colleges, universities, presses, libraries, vendor companies, and research companies largely share a spirit of cooperation and support among practitioners in our fields.

Michele DiPietro is a past president of the Professional and Organizational Development (POD) Network, and at the organization's 2015 annual meeting, he summed up this spirit in a speech accepting the Spirit of POD award:

> It doesn't matter where you are from, whether you are a one-person shop or have twenty people on your staff, whether you work in a tiny two-year school or at a huge Research-1 university or for a vendor. If you see something that someone else in POD has done that would work for you, my advice is simple. We all share our work and our ideas and our commitment to improving the field: drive it like you stole it! (DiPietro, 2015)

In this chapter, we will share some of the groups to which many alt-ac professionals belong and show how membership in such groups can help your alt-ac career path and why an active approach to professional organization membership reaps the best rewards.

Professional Organizations for Alt-Acs

For alt-ac professionals who are pursuing careers within higher education, the following professional organizations and conferences represent large numbers of people in their respective fields.

Faculty Development

- Professional and Organizational Development (POD) Network: podnetwork.org
- Society for Teaching and Learning in Higher Education (STLHE): www.stlhe.ca
- Lilly Conferences: lillyconferences.com
- International Consortium for Educational Development (ICED): icedonline.net

Higher Education Administration

- Distance Learning Administration (DLA): www.westga.edu/~distance/dla
- U.S. Distance Learning Association (USDLA): www.usdla.org
- Society of Research Administrators (SRA) International: www.srainternational.org

Communications, Public Relations, and Marketing

- American Marketing Association (AMA): www.ama.org

Advocacy Groups

- Association of American Colleges & Universities (AAC&U): www.aacu.org

Information Technology and Media

- EDUCAUSE: www.educause.edu

Distance Learning and Online Programs

- Online Learning Consortium (OLC): onlinelearningconsortium.org
- University Professional and Continuing Education Association (UPCEA): upcea.edu
- Quality Matters (QM): www.qualitymatters.org
- WICHE Cooperative for Educational Technologies (WCET): wcet.wiche.edu

For readers pursuing alt-ac careers outside of colleges and universities, the following list of groups is an excellent place to start your networking connections

Consulting and Entrepreneurship

- Institute of Management Consultants (IMC): www.imcusa.org
- American Marketing Association (AMA): www.ama.org
- Entrepreneurs' Organization (EO): www.eonetwork.org
- Ashoka: www.ashoka.org/en

Human Resources and Services

- Society for Human Resource Management (SHRM): www.shrm.org
- Association for Talent Development (ATD): www.td.org
- International Public Management Association for Human Resources (IPMA-HR): www.ipma-hr.org

K–12 Education

- National Education Association (NEA): www.nea.org
- National Council of Teachers of Mathematics (NCTM): www.nctm.org
- American Association of School Administrators (AASA): www.aasa.org

Organizational Management

- Association of Change Management Professionals (ACMP): www.acmpglobal.org

Research and Analysis

- Institute for Operations Research and the Management Sciences (INFORMS): www.informs.org
- Association for Institutional Research (AIR): www.airweb.org/pages/default.aspx

Writing, Publishing, and Editing

- Association of American Publishers (AAP): publishers.org

Government and Public Service

- Partnership for Public Service: ourpublicservice.org
- Young Professionals in Foreign Policy: www.ypfp.org
- Federally Employed Women: www.few.org

Getting Out What You Put In

One thing we can emphasize about involvement in professional organizations is that you get out of them what you put into them. It is easy to sign up for memberships in several groups and then just receive their e-mail messages, newsletters, and other communications. As leaders in several professional organizations ourselves, we see that a significant percentage of the names on our groups' member rolls are people whom we have never seen in person. Don't be that member.

From a financial and a time-given standpoint, it is better to err on the side of joining fewer organizations that really resonate with your professional goals and ideals rather than try to be part of everything in your field. That is the takeaway for this chapter. Even if you attend a number of different events, subscribe to different groups' electronic mailing lists, or follow various organizations on social media, be choosy about to which groups you devote your time and resources. Create a small network of close connections and a larger network of looser connections (Granovetter, 1973). The technical term is *moving beyond homophily* (Rhodes & Butler, 2010), but we call it *alt-ac resource management*.

Professional organizations and the close working relationships that they foster are a primary source for career advice, ideas, and advancement. All three of the authors of this book found positions and work thanks to conversations and connections in their various professional groups, so the investment of time and energy that it takes to avoid being a passive group member is definitely worth it.

We spoke to Hoag Holmgren, the longtime executive director of the POD Network, and asked him what kinds of activities and connections he saw as most valuable for members of the organization. Because the POD Network serves people engaged in professional and organizational development, he shared that the organization's members come from a variety of backgrounds. Some have completed PhD programs in fields aligned with the network, like instructional design or organizational development, while others found their way via a different path.

> Typically, they somehow became fascinated with the meta-level of teaching, en route to what they thought was going to be some kind of research, lab, or tenure-track position in whatever field. Through contact with a teaching-excellence center and through exposure to people in the POD Network, they became exposed to other career possibilities. And then they started getting involved on campus, and doing that kind of work, and learning how to do it, and learning about what it is. I think for a lot of people, the learning is firsthand learning, like it was for me. I don't have a degree in organizational development, but I learned how to do it on the ground, so to speak, when I was working at the Graduate Teacher Program at CU-Boulder as a teaching grad student in English. I think that's the case for a lot of people.
>
> One of the reasons that [members] look forward to going to [the POD Network conference] is because it's the only conference where they don't have to explain to anyone what they do. I think we've all been in that situation, sort of an elevator moment, where someone says, "Oh, you're the assistant director of the teaching center: What do you do?" and there's no way you could possibly describe it before the elevator ride is over. In POD, there is just that mutual recognition and shared understanding of what the work is.
>
> I would say get involved with your campus teaching center, if there is one. And definitely get involved with the POD Network: Try to attend a conference. Try to publish in *To Improve the Academy*. Try to present at the conference. Go to sessions. Get involved with the electronic mailing lists. Become a member.
>
> I had a recent conversation with someone who's a PhD, a very up-and-coming, promising, very active future POD member, and we had a long talk about this exact conversation. He said, "What should I focus on? What's going to be the most important area? Should I focus on grad students; should I focus in technology, assessment?" And I told him to focus on what's really interesting to you, because that's what going to bring the most passion and that's what you're going to be most interested in and

that's probably what you're going to be doing. I don't know which one is most important, but find one that you're really, really interested in, and then do that. He seemed to appreciate that, but it's not the answer he was looking for! (H. Holmgren, personal communication, January 29, 2018)

Next Steps

Identify one professional organization where you would like to make connections and send an e-mail message or reach out via social media to a member of the leadership of that organization. Your message contains one request: To be put in touch with three people in the organization who can tell you more about the group and what it does.

When you talk with the three people, tell them what you do, where you are in the alt-ac career pathway, and what your goals are for your career. Then, ask them to share their own experiences and ideas with you. Expect that you will soon have an opportunity to join a committee, work on a project, or just keep up the connection with your colleagues. What is important is that you approach professional organizations as a way to stay current and connected and as a way for you to give of your time and talents for others first.

This type of networking can stay as small or get as large as you would like it to be. You do not need to be an extraverted schmoozer to create meaningful connections with key colleagues in your field. You decide when you stop asking for more introductions and connections; your network might be 3 people or it might be 30. Know, too, that because of limits on our time and social capacities, close professional connections usually have a maximum number—around 150 people, sometimes referred to as Dunbar's number (Hoffman & Casnocha, 2012)—so it is a saner approach to keep your close professional allies to a manageable number.

PART SIX

BUILDING YOUR ALT-AC
PRESENCE

In Part Six, we help you advance your efforts to connect to alt-ac communities. While Part Five addressed your work and professional activities, Part Six concentrates on outward-facing activities. In particular, we focus on translating your disciplinary knowledge and niche academic skills into a wider range of career options so that you can clearly convey their applicability to potential employers. Practical strategies in Part Six include plotting an incremental pathway, building an intentional portfolio of your experiences, and finding a sponsor or mentoring group to support your efforts. We also cover core elements of personal branding.

24

GETTING EXPERIENCE

In this chapter, you will follow steps to plot an incremental pathway to gain various types of experience that will allow you to grow an alt-ac career and presence.

Methods for Gaining Experience

As you progress throughout your alt-ac career, you will have many opportunities to learn and grow. Choosing which experiences you want to prioritize and devote time to will affect the trajectory of your career and the kinds of positions that you will be eligible for in the future. Many alt-ac positions require gaining a level of experience that cannot happen overnight. In this chapter, we'll offer some examples of incremental steps you can take to gain experience over time and through many different avenues.

Finding Your Learning Sweet Spot

Everyone has different ways that they prefer to learn and gain experience. Here are some possibilities to consider.

Formal Education
Depending on your career goals, you might consider taking a course or two, or even earning another degree, to help you as you progress in your career. There are also certifications you can pursue in subjects like coaching or project management that offer hands-on training and give you experience that you can leverage to keep moving forward in your career.

Informal Education
If you do not need formal credit or credentialing, seeking out informal education experiences through MOOCs, workshops, podcasts, and other methods to learn about new topics is a possibility. Informal education experiences

may not come with hands-on training, but you can build in those opportunities yourself through intentional practice and self-discipline.

Mentoring

One-on-one or group mentoring is another way to gain experience through talking about and processing your professional milestones with others. If there is a particular area where you hope to gain more experience, finding another person who has already learned the ropes is an excellent way to gain knowledge and build your professional network simultaneously. Lois Zachary's (2009) book *The Mentee's Guide* is an excellent resource to prepare yourself and get ideas for finding and working with mentors.

Project-Based Learning

Taking on new projects that stretch your current level of abilities or allow you to practice a new area of interest is another way to learn and gain experience. These projects can be small (low stakes) or large (high stakes), depending on the opportunities that may come your way. Combining project-based learning with a mentoring relationship can strengthen the experience that you gain and may speed up your learning curve.

On-the-Job Training

In addition to taking on new projects, you may have opportunities for on-the-job training from a supervisor or peer or through a unit like human resources. For areas like staff management, finance and budgeting, and strategic planning, there may already be a curriculum that your employer provides to help you gain more experience.

Teaching Others

If you have a little experience in a particular area but want to gain more, teaching others can be a strong motivator. As the saying goes, the best way to learn something is to have to teach it to another person. Consider developing a workshop or short course that you share with others interested in learning about the topic so that you can really dig into the fundamentals of the area where you want to gain more knowledge and experience.

Reading

For some people, reading and research is the preferred method of learning from others when trying to gain more experience in a new area. Although you will eventually have to practice what you are attempting to learn more about to eventually demonstrate that you have the skills and abilities, reading is an excellent preliminary step to get started.

Know Your Why

Understanding your motivation for learning something new or gaining experience in a particular area will be a key component of your success. For example, if you know that gaining more experience in project management will help you earn that promotion that you've been looking for, then that's your larger why. However, gaining experience is not always just about earning more money or getting that new title (although it can help with both). Sometimes it's about challenging yourself to new levels of knowledge and ability so that you stay engaged in your work and not get bored. Whatever your reason for pursuing more experience in a certain area, knowing your motivation for doing so can help you persevere when the going gets tough.

Learning Via the Stepladder Model

Once you have reviewed all the different ways that you can gain experience in a particular area, you can start to build a stepladder of tasks that will lead to you increasing your knowledge and skills. Let's look at some examples.

Grant Writing

If you have never written a grant before, or if you want to gain more experience in grant writing, you might include the following tasks on your stepladder:

- Gather online resources about writing grants in your industry.
- Read articles or books about grant writing.
- Seek out institutional or company-specific grant writing resources such as in an internal workshop or training.
- Find a colleague who is an experienced grant writer and invite that person to coffee to learn about their experience.
- Explore the different mechanisms for grant funding (state, federal, foundations, etc.) to see what might be a fit for your project.
- Look around for a grant writing experience that you can contribute to as a team member rather than taking a lead role.
- Choose a funding opportunity that is a relatively small commitment to test out what you have learned about grant writing.
- As you experience grant writing success, slowly build your pipeline to include larger grants and funding opportunities.

- Begin to mentor others about grant writing.

As you might imagine, all of these steps together might take a period of months or years to complete. However, having a stepladder approach means that you are developing your skills by building on what you have previously learned in smaller, manageable pieces. Let's look at another example.

Emotional Intelligence

If there are areas of your professional identity that do not come naturally to you, such as emotional intelligence (i.e., how to engage in interpersonal communication effectively with empathy and appropriate reactions in a range of situations), you can take a stepladder approach to building your experience and practice in this area. Here are some tasks that you might include:

- Learn more about emotional intelligence through reading blogs, articles, and books.
- Observe others who practice effective emotional intelligence and note the strategies they are using.
- Practice emotional intelligence in small ways such as asking a coworker about a vacation.
- Practice emotional intelligence with friends and family members outside of the workplace.
- Attend a workshop or webinar on emotional intelligence in the workplace.
- Ask a coworker to help hold you accountable with practicing emotional intelligence.

As you think about the different areas where you might want to gain more experience, take some time to break them down into their component parts so that you can see all of the different opportunities you might have for learning. Once you have a list of possible ways to gain more experience, you can build them into your schedule accordingly. You might be able to complete some smaller tasks in the next weeks or months, whereas other larger milestones might be goals that you set to achieve over longer periods of time.

Methods for Gaining Experience Rapidly

If time is not on your side, you may want to consider these more rapid approaches to skill acquisition. Although this is not always recommended if you are pursuing deep knowledge of a subject (some things just take time), we also understand that there may be times in your career when you need to pick up and demonstrate your skills in a particular area more quickly.

Grab the CliffsNotes

In other words, identify the fundamental things that you need to know to be successful. For example, what are the key vocabulary terms or theories that make up the new knowledge or skill set that you are trying to acquire? Talking the talk can help you more quickly walk the walk, especially if you can practice talking about what you are learning with other people already in the know.

Connect What You Need to Know to What You Already Know

Learning new information works best if you can draw relationships between the new knowledge and the knowledge that you already have. Try to make as many connections as you can with what you need to learn and what you have picked up throughout your previous training and education.

Hire a Personal Tutor

Your company wants you to move to Japan in two months to lead the new division there. Sure! Your only problem is you never learned the Japanese language. If this is your situation (or something similar), hiring a private tutor may be better than investing in a language learning software program that may not be personalized to your industry.

Learn What You Need as You Go

Otherwise known as the fly-by-the-seat-of-your-pants method, this is all about picking up the skills you need as you go. This strategy is best if you get dropped in the deep end on a particular project. Rather than try to strategically plan too far in advance, if this is your situation, we recommend just focusing on the next step that's right in front of you to be successful.

Next Steps

This chapter has lots of tips and strategies for deciding *where* you want to gain more experience, *why* you want to gain that experience, and *how* you will gain that experience. As you review the different areas of your professional life, identify one area that you think could be helped by more knowledge, a deepening of skills, or a broadening of abilities. Articulate your why for choosing that area. Then pick one way that you can accomplish that goal in the next week, in the next month, and in the next year.

One of our favorite resources for enhancing your professional skills and deciding what to learn next is Goldsmith and Reiter's (2007) book *What Got You Here Won't Get You There*. Goldsmith and Reiter assume a lifelong-learning philosophy and share different ways to level up your skills to keep progressing and growing throughout your career. They also offer several strategies for identifying possible obstacles that might be holding you back from developing as a professional in your field and provide resources and tips for how to move past the obstacles that you identify. All of us authors are proponents of lifelong learning as well, because we have each shifted careers a few different times as we continue to strengthen our unique skills sets as alt-ac professionals.

If you are interested in how to learn things fast, we also recommend Kaufman (2013), a primer on how to learn anything within about 20 hours. Kaufman reviews principles of effective learning and rapid skill acquisition and offeres concrete examples from everything from yoga, to programming, to windsurfing. If you find yourself wanting to take a deep dive into a new skill set or you are just feeling the pressure to catch up with colleagues, this is a great resource to check out.

25

BUILDING A PORTFOLIO OVER TIME AND WITH INTENTIONALITY

In this chapter, you will identify (a) what artifacts you should plan, create, collect, and share and (b) how to showcase experience in specific areas or types of work you want to pursue in more depth or quantity.

Building a Habit of Documentation

Previously, we discussed how to build your experience, skills, and knowledge over time and in particular areas. In this chapter, we'll be exploring how to showcase the evidence of that experience so that others can see your professional path and abilities. Building a portfolio of professional artifacts takes some planning and intentionality. We'll start by talking about some strategies for building a habit of documentation so that you are collecting the right materials to contribute to your portfolio. We'll then discuss some methods of showcasing your work in public ways so that others can learn about your professional experiences.

Documenting one's work should be a familiar task for many academics. The idea of citing one's sources or tracking the steps of data analysis so that research can be replicated are common tasks in higher education. At the very least, many academics and higher education professionals are familiar with documenting their work through the updating of a CV or résumé. However, we may not be updating these documents as consistently as we should. Building a habit of documentation can begin with keeping a master list of your professional accomplishments, training, credentialing, skill building, presentations, publications, projects, and other milestones along with a record of the dates when each occurred. Once you have this master list, other—and perhaps more creative—forms of documentation can be generated.

One way to build a habit of documentation is to identify the things that you need to be documenting. Here's a short list of the kinds of things that we keep records of in some shape or form:

- Classes taught or workshops facilitated
- Publications of all kinds
- Conference presentations or invited talks
- Institutional consulting clients
- Work products that you may share publicly
- Professional roles and responsibilities
- Professional affiliations or memberships with organizations
- Educational records
- Postgraduate school training and/or credentialing
- Grants received
- Larger multimedia projects (e.g., podcasts)

This list is just a starting point, and there are many different ways to document this kind of work. For example, one of the authors (Linder) is a frequent podcaster. Each of those podcasts has a website with an episode guide, which serves as a way to document the work of the podcast over time. Linder then links to the podcast websites on her CV for anyone who is interested in learning more about those projects.

Once you know the kinds of things that you want to document (and you might want to consider reviewing and updating your list every six months or so), you can begin to schedule in updates to your calendar. At the very least, we recommend monthly check-ins to add any professional accomplishments or milestones to a master CV or résumé so that you are not losing a record of those areas of your professional life as they are being completed. If you are an active alt-ac professional, it can be easier than you might think to lose track of all of the things you are working on, skills you are building, and knowledge you are gaining.

Other forms of regular documentation are journaling, blogging, or any other form of private or public reflection on your professional work. Whether you write down these reflections, audio record them, or create a form of video diary, they can serve as a form of documentation that can be reviewed and synthesized at a later time. For example, during a 30-day writing challenge in 2017, Linder created brief video diaries (all shorter than 5 minutes) about her progress each day. These short videos became a record of her work over the month and allowed her to showcase her work publicly (they were shared in real time on a YouTube channel), be held accountable to the daily work (she also posted them to her social media community), and see at the end of the month a larger picture of what she was able to accomplish in 30 days. Additionally, these videos are now archived online for anyone to view.

Methods of Showcasing Your Work

As you can see from the previous example, technology advances have afforded us a wide range of ways to document our work. In this section, we'll review some of the possible methods of showcasing what you have documented so that others can view your professional accomplishments. Whatever methods you choose to share your work, you will want to consider the audience you are showcasing the work to. This might help you decide the best methods for how to share your work and in what contexts. For example, you might ask yourself the following questions:

- What can I do to share this work in digestible pieces? (This is especially important for large projects with lots of moving parts.)
- How much time will my audience have to digest this artifact of my professional life?
- What can I do to make this professional artifact more enjoyable for my audience to experience?
- What method of showcasing this professional artifact will make me proud of sharing it with my professional network?
- How will this professional artifact potentially help others with their own work or reach similar goals?

Each of these questions can help you choose from the range of different strategies of showcasing your work that we discuss in the following section.

Creating an Up-to-Date Portfolio

There are several different methods for sharing your most up-to-date work with others. As we mentioned before, if you are an active alt-ac professional, then you will have lots of things to share about what you are learning and doing along your career pathway. Here are some possible ways to share about your professional life with friends and colleagues.

CV or Résumé

Having an up-to-date CV or résumé is the building block of your professional portfolio. If you do nothing else to document your work, make sure that this document is updated regularly so that you can use it for seeking promotions, going on the job market, or applying for grants or other awards.

Professional Website

Professional websites are becoming more and more common as web space and storage has become more affordable and website content management systems such as Squarespace, WordPress, and Wix have made websites easier to create and maintain. A professional website is a kind of home base where you can collect your professional artifacts to showcase. This home base can serve as a digital portfolio of your work and can be flexible enough to hold text-based, image-based, and multimedia examples of your projects.

ePortfolio

Similar to a professional website, there are different forms of ePortfolio software that allow you to showcase your work in an organized and themed manner online. In some ways, LinkedIn, the professional social networking platform, is a kind of ePortfolio because it offers you a CV-like model for sharing about your professional experiences. Other ePortfolio software, such as Wix, PortfolioGen, or Pathbrite, offers easy-to-use templates to share your work online without the added responsibility of designing and managing a self-hosted website.

Publication

For those who are looking for more formal documentation methods, publication is the ultimate method of showcasing your work. Formal publications through journals or publishing houses are archived by others and are date stamped so that it's clear when you created a particular professional artifact. Although we don't often think of our publications as steps along our professional road map, they do tell a story, especially over time, about the things that interested us, the questions we were posing, and the problems we have explored over time.

Multimedia

The podcasts and videos mentioned earlier in this chapter serve as examples of the kinds of multimedia artifacts that you can create to share your work. Some researchers are now creating short videos explaining their articles and other publications to make them easier (and less time-consuming) to digest. If you haven't experimented with multimedia creation yet, start by looking around at some of the examples of what others are doing to see what might be a good fit for your own work. It's never been easier to create multimedia artifacts with the basic tools that come built in to your home and/or work computer.

Social Media

Although a bit more ephemeral, social media is another way to build up a portfolio of your thoughts and reflections over time, tweet by tweet, or blog post by blog post. The interesting thing about creating a portfolio of your work via social media is that it is, by default, influenced by those you are networking with online. The conversations that you have, reactions that you receive, and resources that you share all become part of your larger professional brand (more on this in a later chapter).

Archiving Your Work

The previous strategies are all examples of how to share your current work in a portfolio style, but you will also want to find ways to archive older projects. You have a few options with archiving your work: public archives, private archives, or a mix of the two. Many of us already engage in private archiving. These are all of the digital files related to our projects and professional accomplishments that we are storing on our computers, on external hard drives, or in the cloud. These private archives also include our paper file storage of those notes we used to study for our candidacy exams, the drafts of the articles that eventually got published, and other accoutrements from our professional journeys. Often, these private archives will never see the light of day, but they serve the purpose of reminding ourselves of the labor that was involved with our professional accomplishments.

Public archives are those places where others are invited in to explore and review the documentation of your past projects and work. Blogs are a great example of public archives because they describe a professional journey over time and can be read in a narrative fashion from beginning to end. Other forms of public archives include shared data sets, multimedia channels such as podcasts or videos, and social media archives. As we engage more as professionals in online spaces, our *digital footprints* (Fertik & Thompson, 2015) become a form of public archive that contributes to our professional reputations over time.

Next Steps

What are the different ways that you are already documenting and showcasing your professional work? Are there new methods that you have learned about in this chapter that are of interest to you? Do you have professional artifacts that you want to share but haven't known how to get started? As a next step, find some examples of people who you think are showcasing their work well. Study what they are doing that draws you in to their professional journey. Perhaps you can even reach out to them for a brief chat to learn more about their strategies for sharing their professional life with others.

On the basis of this research, map out a strategy for documenting and sharing your work that you can start to implement over the coming months. Consider how you can use different reflections about specific portfolio artifacts to highlight aspects of your work for a variety of potential audiences, such as potential employers, peers at other institutions, or colleagues. Maybe you want to update or create a professional website, start a blog, or experiment with video diaries on a YouTube channel. Having a clear plan will help you ensure that you are building your professional portfolio intentionally and purposefully.

Having a professional website is becoming more of a must than an option for many alt-ac professionals. If you are ready to take your professional portfolio to the next level, secure a domain name, rent some web space, and launch a professional website for yourself. If you already have one, review it with fresh eyes to see what updates it might need to better serve your current professional status and future career aspirations. If you need additional guidance, see Linder's (2018) chapter on building a professional website.

26

FINDING A SPONSOR OR MENTORING GROUP TO HELP

In this chapter, you will create an initial list of people to whom you can reach out for community support.

Finding Community

As you explore what the alt-ac career path means for you, it may feel a bit lonely. Depending on your current role and future career goals, it may not seem that there are many people who do the kind of work that you do or who are embarking on the kind of path that you are following. However, we can say from experience that there are more alt-ac-oriented academics than you might think. Finding a group of colleagues that you can lean on for support and guidance when needed is key.

Seeking Support for the Next Stage of Your Career

One of the more challenging lessons for many alt-acs to learn is that the communities they created for themselves for previous traditional academic roles (as graduate students or as faculty) may not serve them in the alt-ac space. Now, we certainly aren't recommending that you need to abandon all the friends and colleagues whom you hold dear from previous professional or career stages (no need to throw the baby out with the bathwater, as they say), but it is important to realize that as you pursue new career interests and goals, you may need different kinds of support.

Indeed, we touched on this previously in discussions about the limited role that your graduate school adviser might play in your alt-ac job search as compared to if you went on the market for a more traditional tenure-track position. As you explore and grow as an alt-ac professional, we recommend staying open to the possibilities of the communities you might want to seek out, join, or create.

Creating or Joining Groups

There are several different kinds of groups that you might want to consider creating or joining as you continue on your alt-ac career path. Here are several that we have each personally found to be useful along our own pathways.

Mentoring Networks (Including Near Peers)

Mentoring networks are the constellation of people whom you invite to help you grow both personally and professionally. Some of the people in your mentoring network might be local, whereas others are geographically far away. Some may be people who are in your field but have advanced farther than you and can thus offer advice based on their own experiences. Other people in your mentoring network might be what is called a "near peer" (Sorcinelli & Yun, 2007), or someone who is at your level of professional status and who has similar goals or aspirations as you. Each of the people in your mentoring network can provide different resources for you along your professional journey.

Mastermind Groups

Mastermind groups are made up of a small group of colleagues who are looking to support each other through similar professional circumstances. For example, two of the authors (Linder and Tobin) are in a group together for academic small business owners. The goals of a mastermind group can vary, but they often coalesce around two main areas: troubleshooting issues or challenges and providing accountability for taking action. Some mastermind groups begin with check-ins from each member and questions that are asked at every meeting. Other groups are more spontaneous with their agenda. Some best practices for mastermind groups include regular meetings (at least once per month is recommended) and, at the very least, minimal note-taking to track the group's agendas and the group members' accomplishments.

Accountability Groups

Accountability groups might form around a particular set of professional circumstances, but they can also be groups that form around a specific problem or issue that the group members are hoping to address with the help of others. Weight-loss groups are good examples of accountability groups where members attend to receive support and publicly share their challenges and successes. Accountability groups can be both personal and professional and often meet regularly (weekly at a minimum) to ensure that members are keeping up with their goals. Other examples of accountability groups include writing groups and reading groups (more on these next).

Writing Groups

Writing groups have similarities to both mastermind groups and accountability groups. They are focused on helping the group's members complete writing projects and may also include offering feedback on writing pieces. Some writing groups serve only as accountability mechanisms, with members checking in regularly about word counts, minutes written, or other milestones. Other writing groups serve only as places to give and share feedback on writing, with group meetings organized around reading and commenting on one or more group members' work. Some writing groups offer a combination of accountability, feedback, and troubleshooting of writing questions and challenges.

Reading Groups

Reading groups are formed by members who have a similar interest in a particular genre of literature, who are interested in being held accountable to reading more, or who enjoy the social aspects of what is normally a solitary endeavor. Although many reading groups focus on book-length texts, academic reading groups are often formed to share articles or other shorter scholarly works. Like accountability groups, reading groups can be personal or professional and might be hosted at members' homes or in a shared work space or public location, such as a coffee house or restaurant.

Social Media and Online Communities

The social media community for alt-ac professionals is growing (just check out the #altac hashtag for proof). Seeking out other alt-ac professionals on social networks such as Twitter, Facebook, Instagram, LinkedIn, ResearchGate, and Academia.edu can ensure that you won't feel so alone. Additional online communities are forming as member-only groups where alt-acs can receive support, feedback, and knowledge from one another as they pursue their alt-ac careers.

Make Lists

Take a few minutes to think about the best mentors and colleagues you have ever had. Write down their names and consider the following:

- What made them so great?
- How did they support you professionally or personally?
- Do they continue to play an important role in your professional development?

Next, consider the areas of your professional life where you feel unsupported. Maybe these are areas where you are just getting started and don't have much of a network established yet.

Last, write down a list of the people you think you might want to deepen a relationship with. These are the people who might be new mentors for you (near peers or otherwise) or who you think have something important to teach or share with you. As you look at your lists, brainstorm some ways that you might honor the mentors and colleagues who have previously helped you and deepen those relationships with people who are newer to your professional life. Here are some ideas:

- Send a note of thanks to someone on your list to express appreciation for something they have already taught you.
- Create a group like the ones described earlier in this chapter and invite some people to join it with you.
- Invite someone to coffee to learn more about that person and share more about your own pathway.

Next Steps

An excellent example of a mentoring map comes from the National Center for Faculty Development and Diversity (see Rockquemore, 2017) and provides spaces for the following categories of mentors:

- Substantive feedback
- Professional development
- Sponsorship
- Emotional support
- Access to opportunities
- Accountability for what really matters
- Intellectual community
- Safe space
- Role models

We recommend printing a copy of the mentoring network map and filling it out based on your current professional role and future aspirations.

Don't forget to periodically revisit your mentoring map as your professional development goals shift and change directions.

Personal thank-you notes, handwritten if possible, are also one of the best ways that we know for you to strengthen community ties and be memorable to others in your professional network. What you choose to thank people for can be large or small, but the recipient will always be grateful. Find some nice stationery and commit to writing thank-you notes on a regular basis for the next six months to a year. We promise you won't be disappointed in the results.

27

CREATING AND GROWING A PERSONAL BRAND

In this chapter, you will (a) make choices about when, where, and how to build your personal brand via public forums and electronic mailing lists, social media platforms, and personal websites and (b) explore the importance of in-person and live outreach.

What Is a Personal Brand?

Not all academics and higher education professionals feel comfortable with the concept of branding. That's understandable. Branding is often commodified, and many people relate it to the concept of selling—or even selling out. But branding can have a more positive interpretation as well. Rather than thinking about branding as a way of selling a product, we recommend considering branding as a tool through which you can set yourself apart and nurture relationships through building trust.

Other words that we use in higher education that are related to branding—and that might be more palatable for you—are *reputation, credibility,* and *expertise.* The concept of a personal brand is made up of those unique qualities that you bring to your work, to social interactions that you have with others, and to the professional contributions that you make over time. Your personal brand is what you are known for in larger professional circles.

What Do You Want to Be Known For?

When you think about branding from the perspective we just outlined, it becomes clear that you have a personal brand, whether you want one or not. You are probably already known for particular things in professional circles. Perhaps you are always on time with deadlines, you are good at working in groups, or you are perceived to be a hard worker. Others might also see you as someone they can depend on when trying to solve difficult problems, write a persuasive grant, or copyedit a really important document. Think about the things that you are already known for and write them down here.

_____

_____

_____

_____

_____

In addition to the things for which you are already known and that are already contributing to your professional reputation are some ideas you may also have for things that you want to be known for and that are more aspirational. These are the things that you often admire in others and wish that you had as well. Or maybe these are things that you are working toward but haven't quite achieved yet.

Good examples of these traits might be having a reputation for being calm under pressure, for always knowing the right thing to say, or for being one of the go-to experts in your field. Aspirational professional traits can take time to practice and build strength in, but it's helpful to note the ones that you consider to be the most important. Note your aspirational professional traits here.

_____

_____

_____

_____

_____

Where Do You Want to Be Known?

As you make decisions about what you want to be known for, you will also want to think about the areas of your industry where you want to be a key influencer. These areas are probably going to fall into one of two categories. The first category consists of the niche areas where you feel that you are already making a mark (refer back to chapter 15 about finding your niche). These might be areas where you have already started to publish or present on certain theories, techniques, or practices.

The second category includes those areas that you have identified where you can see a strong combination of your skills and abilities with a gap in the field or industry. For example, each time Linder has started a new podcast project (she now hosts or cohosts four shows), it's been because she cannot find another podcast like it. She figured if she wanted a podcast on that topic, others would as well.

Deciding on the places where you want to be known will also help you identify key audiences for building your reputation. Chris Cloney, a recent PhD graduate and dust explosion researcher, found his niche when he started collecting data and sharing information on explosion incidents via a database and weekly newsletter. Chris has an audience of researchers and industry experts who rely on his regular information sharing to create better research and make real-world safety decisions. Chris's newsletter is now sponsored by industry partners as he shares out the latest dust explosion news and industrial safety content. He also produces an annual incident report and maintains a regular blog and podcast, which have helped him build his audience over time.

How Do You Want to Be Known?

In additional to identifying the professional traits or abilities that you want to be known for, and the people with whom you feel you can build an audience, you will also need to identify how people will learn about you. These strategies will allow you to build an audience over time, which is how you can strengthen and grow your larger professional network. There are several different ways that you can go about building a professional reputation through connecting with an audience.

Public Speaking

There may be no better way to build your reputation with large groups of people than speaking in front of large groups of people. Giving keynotes, facilitating workshops or trainings, and speaking at conferences are all excellent ways of sharing your knowledge and skills with others in your field or industry. If you are an effective public speaker and you can make a strong impression on a large group, word will quickly spread about your abilities.

Publishing

Positioning yourself as an expert in your field can also be done through publishing. In academia, and in many other industries, publishing is a career currency that is difficult to match. If you can establish yourself as *the* expert on a particular topic or in a specific area, then your personal brand will get a definite boost.

Blogging

Similar to publishing, but less formal and on a shorter time line, blogging is another excellent way to establish your expertise in your field or in a subfield of your choosing. To build your reputation via blogging, you will need to be consistently posting and marketing your blog to gain a following, but blogging is one of the easiest reputation practices to start. Group blogging platforms like Medium also make it easier to tag your posts for easy sharing with others interested in your area of expertise.

Creating a Newsletter

Producing a regular newsletter with valuable content for a particular audience is another possibility for building your reputation. Like the example with Chris mentioned previously, newsletters can also be a way to generate additional revenue. If you are regular blogger, you can also offer your blog content via e-mail and create a newsletter by reusing that blog content in another medium.

Social Media Engagement

Along the lines of blogging, consistent social media engagement via Twitter, Facebook, LinkedIn, or another platform of your choice can also help build and strengthen your professional reputation. You can become known for being a key expert on a particular topic, or maybe you just build a reputation for always posting incredibly useful resources on a subject or area that you are learning more about.

Electronic Mailing Lists, Discussion Boards, or Other Online Professional Communities

If your field or industry has a public online forum where professionals are posting resources, questions, or job announcements, this is another area where you can be building your reputation and brand. For example, you probably want to be the person who always has a helpful resource rather than the person who is always asking for help from the community without contributing back.

Professional Website

We already discussed the importance of having a professional website, and we'll continue that discussion here. Having a home base online that you can control (after all, Twitter could be gone tomorrow) and where you can curate information about your personal brand and reputation has never been easier. Your professional website can also host a blog if you choose to build your reputation through that kind of platform as well.

Strengthening Your Network (and Your Reputation)

Once you have nurtured your brand and created an audience to share your knowledge with, you will want to make sure you are serving your audience to strengthen your relationship with them and your overall reputation. The most important thing that you can do to maintain and strengthen relationships, and to continue to build trust, is to create a two-way communication channel where your audience hears from you on a consistent basis (through one of the many strategies mentioned previously in this chapter) and also where you can hear from your audience. For example, engaging with those who follow you on social media platforms is one place to start. Ask questions, seek resources, and express gratitude when someone shares helpful content.

This is what invites your audience to become a part of your larger network. Frequent check-ins with your network will allow you to make sure you are on target with the content you are producing so that it remains useful and relevant to those in your network who want to connect with and learn from you.

Next Steps

As you start to make some decisions about when, where, and how to build your personal brand, we recommend starting with a content strategy. Another way to think about a content strategy is to ask yourself what kinds of things you like to talk about on a regular basis and how you like to talk about them. For example, how do you like to discuss productivity tips and how to work more efficiently? That might be a potential content topic for you.

Now, do you prefer to talk about that topic with others? Write about it? And when you do share content with others, what kinds of content do you like to share? Personal experience? Reviews of books and resources? The stories of others? Start to get some details down about your personalized branding strategy. Keep in mind that it's okay if you want to head in a few different directions at once. Building a brand takes time and a certain amount of experimentation before you find the niches that are just right for you.

Want to go deeper into shaping your personal brand? Consider taking Sally Hogshead's "How to Fascinate" personality test. This tool allows you to identify your personal strengths related to how others perceive you when you are at your professional and personal best. This tool is particularly helpful if you are looking for words to help market yourself as a speaker or consultant or if you are going on the job market. Learn more by visiting www.howto fascinate.com or from Hogshead (2014, 2016).

An additional resource on personal branding is Dorie Clark's (2017) *Entrepreneurial You.* Although we certainly don't think that personal branding is important for only entrepreneurs or alt-acs who are self-employed, this book offers a helpful guide to getting started with speaking, podcasting, blogging, and several of the other communication and brand-building methods that we mentioned in this chapter.

PART SEVEN

THE ALT-AC CAREER LIFE CYCLE

art Seven addresses readers who are at the midpoint of their careers, as well as early-career readers looking to plan out a varied path for what is coming next. Unlike the tenure track in higher education, alt-ac positions are seldom a closed-ladder option. Professionals often move in and out of alt-ac positions, building careers among faculty, industry, and alt-ac positions. In Part Seven, we discuss how to move from an alt-ac position to a faculty role and vice versa. We also share best practices about adding a part-time alt-ac component to your full-time work, and this part of this book closes with a deep dive into mentoring to help you establish a pipeline for newer alt-ac professionals.

28

FROM ALT-AC TO
FACULTY ROLES

In this chapter, you will learn how to establish your bona fides for faculty positions while you are still an alt-ac professional in order to make a successful transition to a faculty role.

Getting Ready for Faculty Positions

Although not always the goal, alt-ac work can sometimes be a springboard into a faculty position at a college or university. Many people begin their careers in alt-ac roles because there are relatively few positions open in their subject-area fields. Especially if your master's degree or doctoral degree work focused on teaching and research in your subject area, the alt-ac route can become a productive "boomerang" for a mid-career shift back to a faculty role. Your mid-career search for a faculty position can be aided by alt-ac experience that other candidates won't have, and alt-ac skills make you a better candidate for later moves into administration, such as becoming a department chair or dean. While this chapter covers how to move from alt-ac positions into full-time faculty work, we should acknowledge that this type of transition is rare in colleges and universities today. Alt-ac work alone is rarely enough to merit serious consideration for faculty positions, especially on the tenure line. However, alt-ac work plus teaching and research make for a potent combination (albeit one that is challenging to pull together).

It all starts with treating your alt-ac work as though it were a tenure-line faculty position, especially in terms of getting experience in the categories that faculty-hiring and tenure committees look for, as well as framing your alt-ac skills in language that faculty search committees understand. Because the various levels of the tenure track map generally onto alt-ac career paths, as you saw in chapter 21, if you know that your eventual goal is to move to a faculty position some time during your alt-ac career, you can structure and document your alt-ac work so that you satisfy the requirements for the types of tenure-track positions you might want. Fortunately, this is not as complex as it might sound.

At each stage of the tenure track—from instructor positions to assistant, associate, and full professorships—there are well-established guidelines at nearly every college and university for what faculty members need to do in the areas of teaching, research, and service to achieve promotion. These guidelines are usually available from the institution or from the faculty union, depending on the makeup of the institution. In this chapter, we will use some sample promotion requirements to craft a crosswalk chart, noting which alt-ac job skills map to faculty-hiring skills at each level of the career ladder, as well as some skills that you will need to add to your alt-ac work to be best prepared for a transition to a faculty role.

A Role-Based Skill Crosswalk

Just like for alt-ac positions, the requirements for instructor-level and tenure-track faculty position hiring and promotion vary considerably across disciplines and institutions. However, there are some commonalities among them that allow us to establish a crosswalk list of common requirements.

Alt-Ac Entry-Level and Faculty Instructor Positions

For instructor-level faculty positions, hiring committees usually focus on teaching experience, sometimes to the exclusion of other skill sets. Job descriptions for these types of positions also often include requirements such as experience in designing learning interactions, teaching with technology (from tech-enhanced courses all the way to fully online courses), and some light service experience, such as having served as an academic committee member.

As an alt-ac professional in an entry-level job, if you want to move laterally into an instructor position (or add a part-time instructor position as a side job), document your experience designing interactions for learners. Even if this takes the form of creating multimedia or crafting self-paced training modules, it is relevant to a faculty position. Likewise, collect information about any teaching or facilitation you have done.

Of course, teaching credit courses for a college or university would top such a list and include things like workshop facilitation, industry-based training sessions, and peer engagement facilitation. In alt-ac positions where you are able to serve on projects or committees with tasks and duties that expand beyond your usual job expectations, show how your role contributed to the overall success of the company or project.

We often do not make time to quantify the work that we do as alt-acs. Collect statistics about the number of consultations you do, the number of people who call or e-mail you for assistance, and the number of hours you spend in a month on project work or doing teaching and training. Also collect testimonials from people whom you've served and from your supervisors. Having external reviewers of your work will be a foundation of your faculty position application packet.

Alt-Ac Associate and Faculty Assistant Professor Positions

If you have been in your alt-ac career for a few years and want to obtain a faculty position at the assistant professor level, expect that hiring committees will look for the following levels of experience. This sample is from the University of Chicago.

> *Letters from the Chair or Dean.* How has the candidate moved beyond the original dissertation research? What significant new scholarly contributions has the candidate made? What is in the pipeline? . . . [Has] enough work been published for experts to gauge the candidate's impact on the field?
> *Letters from Outside Referees.* At the earliest stages of a career, although outside letters are of limited value, we expect them in all cases. Three to four letters will usually suffice.
> *Evidence of Teaching Effectiveness.* We wish to understand both the extent and the quality of the candidate's teaching. Evidence of effective teaching cannot reasonably be expected in all cases for early-career appointments. Chairs/Deans should request evaluations from the candidate's institution, if at all possible. When there is evidence, it should be included and analyzed. If students have participated in the selection of a new appointment, departments may wish to invite them to contribute letters stating their impressions. (Office of the Provost, 2018)

Note that assistant professor positions are the most open to people making a transition from alt-ac to tenure-track faculty work, because such positions are intended as entry points into the faculty profession.

Alt-Ac Coordinator and Faculty Associate Professor Positions

For alt-ac professionals in mid-career (say, with 10 or more years of alt-ac work experience), associate professor positions can be a good next step. Know that most associate professor jobs go to people who have served in an assistant professor capacity, so it is more challenging to come into academia at the associate professor level without a substantial body of work behind you.

TABLE 28.1
Alt-Ac to Associate Professor Skill Chart

Alt-Ac Skills	*Associate Professor Skills*
Evidence of multiple years of effective training, peer mentoring, and teaching in your alt-ac field.	Demonstrated commitment to teaching work of high caliber.
National reputation within your alt-ac field, especially as it relates to research or professional development.	Established national reputation as a scholar and researcher.
Multiyear record of service to your company or institution, with increasing levels of responsibility and leadership.	Service in college or university affairs at the department level.
Service to academic institutions or professional organizations in positions of strategic importance or leadership.	Public, professional, or university service outside departmental responsibilities.

Table 28.1 shows examples of cognate skills in alt-ac positions that can meet the typical associate professor requirements, which can be helpful to keep in mind as you prepare to make the transition.

Alt-Ac Director and Faculty Full Professor Positions
It is rare for full professor positions to be awarded to people who did not come up through the academic tenure process. However, for senior alt-ac practitioners who also have significant teaching, research, and academic service experience, a professorship can be a rewarding cap to your career ladder.

Expect that hiring committees will want to see significant leadership and publication experience in the academic field (Committee on Appointment and Promotions, 2017). This usually translates to (a) at least one book published (in the humanities) or peer-reviewed articles in highly ranked journals and grants obtained (in the sciences) and (b) a leadership role held for several years either in a college or university or with a professional organization that directly serves the academic field. You will also want to consider institutional context. For example, at Research-1 (R1) institutions, teaching may become less of a deciding factor (Faculty Senate, 2008), with research taking priority (and, implicitly, the ability to obtain grants and bring in other research-based funding). For seasoned alt-ac professionals who have established large and well-funded research projects, this can provide an opportunity for them to move into a research-based faculty position to continue their research agenda.

Faculty Skills Not Usually Obtained in Alt-Ac Work

Although this skill crosswalk demonstrates that there are many skill sets that are prized for faculty positions, some are not usually part of alt-ac work. You should plan to add these skills to your alt-ac work or look for separate opportunities to demonstrate these skills outside of your alt-ac work.

Credit-Based College or University Teaching

In many alt-ac positions, teaching happens all the time but not in a way that is easily quantifiable. For better or for worse, faculty-hiring committees tend to set aside candidates who do not have at least some experience teaching credit-based courses at the college level. This is perhaps one of the easier "holes" to patch in your résumé, because most colleges and universities have part-time and one-time openings for practitioners to teach introductory-level courses in their fields.

The bonus of teaching courses, in addition to adding lines to your employment dossier, is that you have access to the teaching and learning center staff or other support staffers whose job is to help you craft the best course you can. If your schedule permits, take advantage of the course design support from the college or university where you teach. Those staffers can then write support letters for you that talk about your adult learning and course design skills.

Subject Matter Publication

Most of us came up through our graduate studies specializing in niche subsets in our fields, and the move to alt-ac work often entailed dropping our subject matter expertise and refocusing on the practical skills in our alt-ac positions. When committees are looking to hire faculty members, they want to see a track record of publication in the field of study—more like the types of expectations for which our graduate programs traditionally prepare us.

Because alt-ac work either (a) does not explicitly require or reward publication or (b) creates research and publication opportunities in our alt-ac fields and not our original scholarly fields, you can get creative in establishing a track record of faculty-focused publication. For instance, many faculty positions value scholarship about the teaching process (called *scholarship of teaching and learning*, or SoTL) in the field or discipline. So, even if you are not using your medieval history degree directly as a museum director, you can still perform research and publish in the area of how best to teach medieval history, especially if you are teaching a course or two already to establish your teaching bona fides. For those of you whose alt-ac careers and family responsibilities leave little time for scholarship, just paying attention to the way that your own courses are going, collecting data about your students' outcomes in response to various teaching techniques and innovations, and writing the results for publication (Faculty Affairs Office, 2018) can be an effective strategy to show your academic publication chops. Be aware, too, of what is considered most important for the discipline and context in which you want to be: In some disciplines, there is no substitute for things like in-field research, grant seeking, or collaborative publication.

Service to Academia

In our alt-ac roles, we often perform committee work, join and contribute to professional organizations, and take an active part in the professional life of our alt-ac fields. When you contemplate a move to a faculty position, it is crucial to identify the areas of overlap that demonstrate service in an academically meaningful way. Project and committee work in professional organizations often fit this requirement. While you are employed in an alt-ac field, look for opportunities to give back to specific academic units, such as serving as an external reviewer for a PhD candidate's dissertation, consulting with an academic department on projects, or serving ex officio on a college or department governing board or fund-raising campaign (Committee on Promotion Tracks, 2015).

The common theme among all of these elements that are not usually part of alt-ac work is their narrow focus on the academic environment. The more clearly you can establish a link between your alt-ac experiences and the typical kinds of skill sets for which college and university hiring committees are usually looking, the better your chances are of landing a faculty position. There is also a silver lining to this "extra" effort: Your alt-ac skills are an added bonus that few people who have held only faculty positions are likely to have obtained, so you can package yourself as having the core skills plus expert-level additional experiences and attributes.

Next Steps

One of the common tasks for faculty members who want to be hired or promoted is to put together a tenure packet or dossier that shows evidence of their teaching, scholarship, and service. In some alt-ac positions there is not as detailed a requirement to document your work and achievements.

Your first step when contemplating the switch from alt-ac work to a faculty position is to think like a faculty review committee as you craft a sort of alt-ac dossier. Such a dossier might contain sections like the following (see Kelsky, 2011):

- Summary statement
- CV
- Publications list
- Teaching portfolio
- Grants and awards list
- Evidence of service
- External review letters

The alt-ac dossier that you create will mirror the format of the tenure-line packet requirements at the college or university where you wish to make your transition. The biggest difference in applying for a faculty position versus another alt-ac job is in the tone and approach. Instead of emphasizing the administrative or operational aspects of your career, play up your experience in teaching, research, and service to the profession, with your traditional alt-ac strengths included as elements that will make you a more well-rounded faculty member—and, if you are so inclined, a better candidate for a later administrative role such as department chair or dean. The final step is to ask a colleague who works in the type of position you want to review your dossier and help assess your employability.

29

FROM FACULTY TO
ALT-AC ROLES

In this chapter, you will learn whether—and when—it is appropriate to leave an existing established academic position for an alt-ac career and how to make that transition.

Decisions, Decisions

A growing number of us who were trained for tenure-line faculty jobs end up teaching or doing research in academic positions that are not on the tenure line: part- and full-time instructor-level work that pays the bills but that does not come with the security of the tenure process (Griffey, 2017). Later, in chapter 30, we will look at how to mix teaching, research, and alt-ac roles on a part-time basis. In this chapter, we will show you how to put your faculty experience to good use when you decide to switch to an alt-ac role (and how to keep the door open if you want to switch back later on in your career, as you saw in chapter 28).

After you have established your academic career in a faculty position, your decision to make the move to an alt-ac space can be motivated by many factors. If you move to a new city because your partner gets a new position, and there are no faculty positions open (e.g., Chohan, 2016), necessity dictates looking more broadly. Likewise, if you are dissatisfied with your current work environment or if you become interested in the work done in an alt-ac field, those become good motivators as well.

Ruth Nemire made the leap to an alt-ac leadership position for a national association after gaining years of combined experience as a practitioner in her field, a faculty member, and a campus leader. Before, during, and after earning a professional doctorate degree in pharmacy (PharmD), she worked as a pharmacist. After graduating, she taught for the University of Miami, then acted as the director of the Center for Neurology Studies at Texas

Tech, and then became the director of community engagement for the Nova Southeastern University College of Pharmacy.

About 10 years after earning a PharmD degree, Nemire went back to school to earn an EdD degree as well. While she finished her doctoral studies in education, she became associate dean at Touro College of Pharmacy. Soon after she graduated, she became the executive founding dean and a professor for Fairleigh Dickinson University. Having built a considerable network along with her experience, she served the American Association of Colleges of Pharmacy for over 6 years in several leadership roles that built toward her final position as senior vice president and chief academic officer for the American Association of Colleges of Pharmacy. She now leads ASK Educational Games, LLC, as its CEO and cofounder.

A Numbers Game

Unlike the process of going from alt-ac work to faculty positions that you read about in chapter 28, moving in the reverse direction often does not require much extra preparation on your part beforehand. The challenge here is to recast your teaching, scholarship, and service experience into language that alt-ac hiring managers will understand and appreciate. Here, the name of the game is quantification. For every type of interaction that we have as faculty members with materials (research), students (teaching), colleagues (service), and the wider world (outreach), begin to count and track the number and scope of each.

Note the number of instances; the total participants; the amount of funds earned, applied, and overseen; and any supervisory or team-based leadership roles you have played. For instance, Tobin keeps a list of all of the courses he has taught. When he applied to work on the internal learning and development team at Blue Cross and Blue Shield, he translated teaching over 1,000 students into project management and teamwork skills.

Often, our PhD programs do not prepare us well for jobs other than being faculty members; however, the silver lining is that being faculty members often prepares us very well for alt-ac work. In many alt-ac fields, including teaching center, museum, publishing, public relations, marketing, and administration, the core job skills match up well with the types of tasks that we do in faculty work—we just call them different things.

Translating Faculty Work Into Alt-Ac Job Skills

Just like for faculty work, the requirements for alt-ac hiring and promotion vary considerably across fields and institutions. Alt-ac jobs share a number of

TABLE 29.1
Faculty to Alt-Ac Skill Chart

Faculty Expectations	Cognate Alt-Ac Skills
Course teaching work	Training, peer mentoring, event facilitation, project management, teaching
Scholarly research	Written and verbal communication skills, writing for specific audiences, project management, talent development
Committee and service work	Leadership, teamwork, project management, budgeting, technology integration
Public, professional, or university service outside departmental responsibilities	Strategic planning, interaction with the public, community relations, event planning, networking

skill sets in common, however. The crosswalk shown in Table 29.1 displays common names for faculty work and translates them into alt-ac job skill categories.

Note how being able to quantify your skills allows you more easily to talk about how your faculty skills can apply in alt-ac positions.

Next Steps

Coming from a faculty position into alt-ac work allows you to present your teaching, service, and research experiences as a solid foundation on which to build (McGinn, 2016), especially if your alt-ac position is still within higher education, such as with a teaching center or university press. Having been a faculty member is a valuable asset for people who work with academics on a regular basis.

A first step is to quantify your work as a faculty member—something that those of us not on the tenure line might not be asked to do—and then translate it into alt-ac language, especially as it relates to the specific job in which you are interested.

30

PART-TIME ALT-AC ROLES

In this chapter, you will (a) determine your ideal side-work combination and area and (b) learn how to allocate time and resources to an alt-ac role while honoring other work and family commitments.

The Side Gig Economy

In today's economy, having a side gig has become a legitimate expectation even for people early in their careers. In fact, economists estimate that in 2020, the "gig economy" is roughly 40% of the U.S. workforce—made up of both full-time freelancers and part-time freelancers who have a side gig (Gillespie, 2017). Academia is following a larger trend of people incorporating a side hustle into their work. However, unlike the average Uber or Lyft driver earning only $210.00 a month (Bhattarai, 2017), alt-ac side work can be a significant financial addition to what you earn in your full-time academic job.

Also, the reputation of alt-ac work has changed, especially since 2010. It used to be that people doing alt-ac work part-time were either retired academics who decided to consult before they retired fully (Zipkin, 2015) or people who had washed out of the higher education job market and turned to consulting to scrape together a living. In chapters 28 and 29, you read about many of the expectations of faculty members on the tenure track—things like giving professional presentations, achieving prominence in one's field, and publishing about one's scholarship. In addition to being ways to "check the box" for a tenure and promotion application, all of these pursuits can be productive, fulfilling, and financially rewarding part-time alt-ac work.

Especially for those of us who hold advanced degrees and work outside of academia, taking on a part-time alt-ac role often makes sense. One of the most common alt-ac side gigs is teaching as a lecturer or adjunct. A wide variety of people with terminal degrees teach part-time—often only one or two classes per academic term—while working in nonacademic or nonteaching, alt-ac staff positions. If you have experience teaching online, you will find part-time teaching opportunities around the world, rather than being limited to your geographic location.

Consulting with colleges and universities in your areas of academic expertise is another flexible sideline that can grow or shrink along with your available time to devote to the practice. A 2018 search on HigherEdJobs.com revealed more than 300 part-time consulting situations open for applications. Barebones consulting, as you saw in chapter 20, requires little more than a web presence and a brochure to list your usual subjects and working conditions. Professional experience outside of academia is also a plus for consultants—play up your business knowledge and network with colleagues in your industry who may be able to connect you back to colleges and universities in your local area.

On the flip side, if you have worked or are working as a staff member at a higher education institution, you can parlay that expertise into consulting work as well. Colleges and universities sometimes view consultants with skepticism and value working with people who have inside experience with the culture of higher education.

Another part-time, alt-ac skill area is in the publishing and editing world. Authors and university presses are always looking for people who can read, comment on, edit, and index specialist writing, and such work can flex to match your availability. Some resources in this area include the following:

- Editorial Freelancers Association (www.the-efa.org)
- American Society for Indexing (www.asindexing.org)

One more area of interest for part-time, alt-ac people is in library and information science work. Librarian positions usually require a master's degree in library science, but part-time library positions are often a good fit for people with advanced subject degrees, and there is a broad variety of opportunities in both academic and public library systems, albeit in a lower pay range than for faculty or academic staff careers. In the information science field, digital humanities, health informatics, data visualization, and data management are all areas where alt-acs with good experience can be very successful.

Next Steps

In 2016, Joyce Locke Carter gave the chair's address to the National Council of Teachers of English (NCTE) Conference on College Composition and Communication (CCCC). Carter made a passionate appeal for including multiple paths for new members of the profession:

> We have taken steps to ensure inclusivity without regard to rank, tenure, job title, or type of institution. We feature undergraduate research posters, a graduate student on the EC [Executive Council], a thriving cross-generational (XGEN) initiative, and SIGs [special interest groups] for grad students and retired professors. The program includes papers and roundtables from graduate students, adjunct and contingent faculty, tenure-track faculty, non-academic or "alt-ac" practitioners—from private institutions, two-year, four-year, regional universities, and R1s. (Carter, 2016, p. 380)

Your next step, should you want to pursue alt-ac work on top of your full-time commitments, is to decide where you want to fit into the existing or emerging structures that support and surround people with advanced knowledge in their fields: professional organizations, colleges and universities themselves, museums, libraries, nonprofits, and the like. Follow the networking and communication ideas from chapters 15 and 19 and get the experience of working on your alt-ac life to determine the right balance.

31

BE AN ALT-AC MENTOR

In this chapter, you will learn how to (a) use mentoring as a means of staying connected and paying forward the assistance you received from your own mentors, (b) find mentees, (c) explore fundamental mentorship principles, and (d) support up-and-coming professionals by sharing alt-ac knowledge.

Alt-Ac Mentoring

In the cogent article "From All Sides: Rethinking Professionalization in a Changing Job Market," Ball, Gleason, and Peterson (2015) from Princeton University argued that mentoring is the key to the creation of new norms for the alt-ac field:

> The more we can validate . . . training and mentorship, and create and sustain programming that simultaneously prepares students for traditional *and* related careers, the better. . . . Some might ask whether this is just more work for an already beleaguered faculty. Not if we also empower graduate students themselves to organize and mentor one another in these forums. (p. 108)

We should start seeing graduates of our advanced degree programs who have found alt-ac success become resources, experts, and mentors for others—and we should start relying on them to do so. And we who become successful alt-ac practitioners should become mentors to others. We should not leave this role solely to our faculty colleagues advising graduate students (as we argued in chapter 10).

Regardless of your starting point, whether you are just beginning your alt-ac career, you are an established alt-ac professional, or you are thinking about becoming an alt-ac practitioner, peer mentoring is a key means of keeping up to date, staying connected, and giving back to the field.

Advisers and Mentors

In many graduate programs, faculty members act in a formal capacity to advise their graduate students about the options available to them after they earn their degrees (Conway, 2005). Traditionally, such advising is focused on work within the academy, especially faculty positions. Today, many thinkers advocate for mentoring and advising that takes into account the rich variety of alt-ac positions for which graduate study prepares us.

If you are in a position to advise newer members of your profession, follow the advice of James Van Wyck of Fordham University and a member of the Graduate Career Consortium. We paraphrase Van Wyck's advice as follows:

- Follow the process set down by successful mentors and advisers who came before you. For example, see the University of Michigan's guide to mentoring (www.rackham.umich.edu/downloads/publications/Fmentoring.pdf).
- Acknowledge that alt-ac work is valuable. Just sharing your own "awareness and approval of . . . non-professorial employment" helps bring alt-ac work into the sphere of the possible.
- Do the research. Visit with professionals in various fields, especially with graduates of your own programs who have gone on to alt-ac positions. Find out what brought them there and what keeps them there, and compile you own list of contacts for current mentees.
- Network. Social media networks like LinkedIn and professional organizations are excellent places to tap into the collective experience of our colleagues, who can become resources for us and our mentees (Van Wyck, 2018).

Next Steps

If your institution assigns you to a formal adviser or mentor role, that is splendid. But you need not be in a formal relationship to share your ideas about alt-ac work (Phillips, 2009). Informal mentoring is often the first type of outreach in which aspiring alt-ac people engage—perhaps because of the dearth of formal avenues for exploring alt-ac careers.

It is one reason why we wrote this book, and we hope that this trend is changing to include more and broader options for formal mentoring and advising. One of the authors, Kelly, has acted as an informal "ghost adviser" in his department for over a decade (even though he's a part-time lecturer). The graduate students want to ask questions that someone who has worked outside higher education can answer.

The fundamental principles of mentoring and advising others, once you yourself have engaged in alt-ac work, are simple ones. Anthony Grafton and James Grossman (2011) advocated for telling PhD students that their degree will "open a broad range of doors" (para. 9) through making some positive changes. We endorse their three-changes model as a way for you to reach out to newer members of your own profession:

> Change our attitudes and our language, to make clear to students entering programs in history that we are offering them education that we believe in, not just as reproductions of ourselves, but also as contributors to public culture and even the private sector. . . .
>
> Examine the training we offer, and work out how to preserve its best traditional qualities while adding new options. . . .
>
> Keep dissertation writers attuned to the full range of opportunities that their work opens. . . . Consider workshops that explore the world of work, bring in speakers from government and other areas where many historians find jobs, and mobilize networks of contacts as advisers for students.
>
> Make clear to all students that they will enjoy their advisors' and their departments' unequivocal support, whether they seek to teach at college or university level, join a non-profit agency or head off into business or government. (Grafton & Grossman, 2011, paras. 10–14)

As a mentor or adviser, strive to help your colleagues make informed decisions about their career steps. Help them find data, people, and experiences that will encourage them to see how their skills can be put to good use not just in faculty positions but in varied and rewarding alt-ac areas. If you find yourself in a mentoring relationship and want to grow in that capacity, get a copy of *The Mentor's Guide* by Lois Zachary (2011).

CONCLUSION

In this conclusion, you will create your next steps based on the alt-ac path you have determined through the examples, advice, and interactions throughout this book.

Ending at the Beginning

Our book ends where it began, with the following question: Where will you go from here? Now that you have learned more about alt-ac careers and roles, and now that you have seen examples of people who have crafted their own alt-ac careers in various ways, it is time to map your next steps on your own alt-ac path. As you begin to formulate your next steps toward going alt-ac, we'd like to share the following opportunities that successful alt-ac practitioners consider in their careers:

- Creative opportunities
- Asking for opportunities
- Professional development opportunities
- Changing opportunities
- Welcoming opportunities
- Challenging opportunities
- Outside-the-box opportunities
- Value opportunities

Each of these areas of alt-ac career preparation, development, and sustaining helps you think and plan in concrete ways. As a final exercise, read this conclusion with a pen and paper handy or your notes application open. To help with this process, we want to introduce you to Todd Zakrajsek. We talked to him in 2018, and, as you will see, his career path touches on all eight of these alt-ac opportunities. As you read, distill your responses from previous exercises throughout the book, and commit to one concrete first step for each area of opportunity.

Successful Alt-Acs Get Creative With Opportunities

As you read about in chapters 3 and 4, alt-ac positions are so varied that there isn't a single path to follow or source of information for where to look to see what opportunities even exist. Many of us started out on a traditional academic path and then realized that it led to possibilities that were much more limited than we'd wanted. Early on, Zakrajsek and his spouse experienced the two-body problem that we talked about in chapter 14.

> Here's how I began my path toward becoming an alt-ac professional. I earned my degree in industrial psychology. My wife wasn't done [with her graduate studies] yet, and I didn't want to be place-committed, forcing her to attend whatever program was nearby. I told her to pick a degree and a place where she wanted to study, and I would find adjunct teaching in that area. During that time I ended up teaching at a large university and a private college, and extended degree programs in another city. I spent 2 years driving 40 hours a week to teach adjunct for $17,000 a year, at a time when typical assistant professor salaries were about $35,000. What it gave me was a glimpse into how an academic road prof feels: underpaid and frequently excluded from the department/campus community. This included being nominated for teaching awards only to be told "We only give teaching awards to full-time people, not part-time people." (T. Zakrajsek, personal communication, January 15, 2018)

Zakrajsek and his spouse worked together to ensure that they could both move toward their goals. The creative solution they discovered was to use their skills to support one another while they both completed their studies. Zakrajsek's spouse worked as a nurse while he completed his degree, and he picked up teaching courses while she completed her degree. Even though Zakrajsek's early career wasn't immediately an alt-ac one, he was willing to find a solution outside of a traditional full-time tenure-track position to help set up longer term goals. Take a moment and write down one long-term goal that you want to accomplish, and list up to five creative ways that you can get the experience and skills that you want to obtain—or ways that you can accommodate practical needs now to set up opportunities in the near future.

Successful Alt-Acs Ask for Opportunities

In chapter 15, we talked about how to find a niche and an audience. That can sound like a huge amount of work, especially if you think about the end goal of making a name for yourself in a field. Fortunately, you don't have to think in such grand terms. Among all of the alt-acs whom the authors of this book know, a surprising majority discovered their niche in an organic way, creating opportunities for themselves by working in directions that intrigued them and then asking for support from their colleagues.

The next phase of Zakrajsek's career exemplifies this. Once his spouse had obtained her graduate degree, he obtained a tenure-track position in the psychology department at a small regional state university.

> I was talking to a friend who had just started promoting the value of active, engaged learning. We set up monthly open brown-bag discussions, and 19 people showed up—which, out of about 200 faculty members, represented roughly 10% of the faculty. I went to the provost and asked if I could I have some money to start an effort to expand similar conversations. The provost said that they had tried something like that a couple of years ago and the faculty were just not interested. I said, "Well, if I start doing it, would you just not stop me?" And the provost said, "Okay." From that point forward I split my attention between teaching and helping others to be better teachers. (T. Zakrajsek, personal communication, January 15, 2018)

However, just being open to alt-ac opportunities is seldom enough to launch your career. As we can see in Zakrajsek's example, the seeds of a faculty development center were there in the informal conversations that he and his colleagues were having about active learning techniques. Even though his provost didn't fund the effort at the beginning, Zakrajsek asked for permission to continue and expand. That conversation gave him room to explore and experiment.

Look at your notes and think about the people who are doing the types of work you want to do or people who could give you permission, resources, or space to explore new ideas. List up to three people to whom you will commit to writing or calling in the coming weeks to talk with about opportunities that you are interested in. And don't forget that "no" to an initial question is often a prelude to "yes" to an alternative.

Successful Alt-Acs Look for Professional Development Opportunities

Chapters 18 and 19 dealt with how to establish credibility and have productive conversations when one is early in one's alt-ac career. The focus of chapter 23 was on using professional organizations to network and find areas for expanding your involvement in alt-ac fields. For instance, Zakrajsek reached out early on to find opportunities in his new field.

> I went to a Lilly Conference and made it a goal to meet and speak to Milton Cox and Laurie Richlin. Milt said, "You know, what you're doing is called faculty development. You need to go to POD." I didn't know what POD was, but I learned, and then I attended my first POD Network conference

[see chapter 23]. The next year, I started a faculty development center at my university and within 2 years had an annual budget of $20,000 and a one-course release. The following year, I got promoted to associate professor, and I got tenured—mostly based on what I was doing with faculty development. I also quickly became immersed in Lilly Conferences and the POD Network, including running for the POD Core Committee just as soon as I was eligible. (T. Zakrajsek, personal communication, January 15, 2018)

As you think about how you want to establish your alt-ac career, take a few minutes and do a key word search online to find one professional organization in your alt-ac area of knowledge. Commit to contacting the organization to connect with a colleague and seek out opportunities to network and collaborate.

Successful Alt-Acs Are Open to Changing Opportunities

In chapter 21, we introduced the idea of advancing your career either by building continuity with one organization or by moving to a different organization—and how to read the signs that will tell you which path to take. Even though he had tenure at a state university, Zakrajsek's provost and president, two of his strongest supporters, informed him they were leaving for other institutions. Anticipating their departure, he knew he would lose support and decided that pursuing faculty development work meant he needed to leave for another university.

In 2001, I applied for a job at another university to start a center for teaching and learning. I rescinded tenure and moved east, even though I very much liked the position I was holding. After three years at this new position, things were proceeding well, and the provost decided to combine learning technologies and faculty development—the thing I was doing. My budget went from $150,000 to about $800,000, and my staff went from one to six full-time people. I learned what it was like to run a learning-technologies group along with faculty development. This position also allowed me the opportunity to facilitate faculty development workshops at campuses throughout the [United States], which both expanded my skills and supplemented my salary. (T. Zakrajsek, personal communication, January 15, 2018)

Whether you are just starting your alt-ac career, moving to or from a traditional faculty position, or thinking about doing alt-ac work to supplement your established work (see chapter 20), list up to three ways in which your work, ideas, or field have changed in the past three years. Zakrajsek was ready to take advantage of the changing nature of how institutions prepared faculty members for the classroom, stepping into the then-nascent field of faculty development. Risk has both negative and positive aspects: Which of the changes you identify has a clear opportunity for you to take a risk in order to obtain a good outcome?

Successful Alt-Acs Welcome Opportunities From Others

In chapters 24 through 27, you learned about how to build an alt-ac portfolio in an intentional way and find sponsors and mentoring groups who can help you develop your career and create a personal brand. One of the key lessons to take away from this book is that being an alt-ac means being part of a team. Even more than in some traditional academic career paths, alt-ac people create their own community. Zakrajsek discovered this when an old friend offered him a unique opportunity.

> Laurie Richin decided to stop directing some of the Lilly Conferences; she had been directing many throughout the U.S. I was offered an opportunity to direct one of the conferences, something I had never considered doing before. Both Laurie and Milt Cox were extremely helpful and supportive in helping me get started as a conference director. About this same time, a position opened at UNC [the University of North Carolina]. Ed Neal, a longtime friend, told me I would be perfect for the position. I was unsure, and Ed convinced me to at least apply and see what would happen. I ended up being offered the position as the executive director of the center, on a campus with nearly 3,000 faculty members. I had a $1.2 million budget, but this was 2008, which was a tremendously fiscally challenging time, resulting in a need to make drastic budget cuts. I also helped to transform the center from a focus on teaching to a Center for Faculty Excellence. We added scholarly endeavors and then leadership support and hired several people. (T. Zakrajsek, personal communication, January 15, 2018)

All of the authors of this book have benefited from opportunities that they hadn't purposefully set up as such. For instance, in 2016, Tobin did a favor for the organizers of the Distance Teaching and Learning conference at the University of Wisconsin–Madison by helping them identify and invite expert speakers on the topic of accessibility and inclusive design. In 2017, they invited him to work for the university as the part-time program chair for the conference, and he is now a full-time remote program area director responsible for an annual conference and curriculum oversight for a professional development certificate program. Take a moment to think about the collaborations and conversations that you have with others in your field and how you might keep those relationships fresh. Write down the names of three colleagues whom you will commit to contacting in order to collaborate with or even just talk with about their experiences and needs.

Successful Alt-Acs Learn From Challenging Opportunities

Alt-ac professionals often build careers that rely on varied skills (see chapters 20, 22, and 30), and we are especially resilient when challenges and barriers crop up. The lesson to take away is that obstacles tend to come up quickly, and being well prepared—or, as it was in Zakrajsek's case, well situated—to respond to unexpected events is a key attribute to cultivate.

> In the UNC Center for Faculty Excellence, I worked with two different directors across three years and got along great with both of them, but they both left sooner than expected: one for health reasons, and the other person for administrative reasons. The third director came in wanting to build his own team, and I was terminated in 2013. The workshops I had started doing several years prior were really starting to take off, and I was at that time running two conferences, so I had planned to stay in Chapel Hill and do workshops and run conferences until my youngest daughter graduated.
>
> Soon after I found myself unemployed, a colleague in the UNC medical school called me and noted, very diplomatically, that a position in faculty development was being created in the medical school. I applied and became the executive director of the medical school's Academy of Educators. Oddly enough, on my CV, there is no gap. I went to UNC as executive director of the Center for Faculty Excellence, held that position for three and a half years, and then became the executive director of the Academy of Educators in the School of Medicine at the same university. (T. Zakrajsek, personal communication, January 15, 2018)

As you think about your alt-ac work, perform a "premortem" analysis. List up to four people, organizations, or groups who offer the most support for your alt-ac studies, work, or career. For each, write down how you would respond if those resources were to diminish or disappear. Doing sound contingency planning is a good use of your time, even if you never have to rely on it (and we hope your challenges will be small, few, and seldom).

Alternately, reflect on a challenge that you have already faced: How did you make it to where you are now, and who helped you recalibrate things? What lessons do you take away from your experiences?

Successful Alt-Acs Consider Outside-the-Box Opportunities

In chapter 16, you read about how to apply your discipline-specific knowledge to a wide range of alt-ac employment opportunities. In many instances, outside-the-box opportunities come along thanks to your curiosity about how your discipline intersects with industry, government, philanthropic organizations, nonprofit companies, or other parts of the college and university hierarchy. Zakrajsek's expansion into faculty development consulting is an excellent example of this.

> Until 2013, my entire career had been full-time alt-ac work in academe. There was an article written in the *American Psychological Observer* years ago [see Polka, 2003] about psychologists who are in nonpsych areas but using their psych degrees—they wrote an article about me and other colleagues. I was doing faculty development using psychology, but not in psych. (T. Zakrajsek, personal communication, January 15, 2018)

Zakrajsek was also expanding his individual consulting work ("I got to thinking that I could make a bigger impact on academe working at many campuses than I could being full-time at one place"). He also became involved in the planning and running of additional Lilly Conferences. He made the conscious decision to reduce his university responsibilities to focus more on those efforts.

> I began in the School of Medicine full-time. Over several years, I gradually reduced my appointment to 85%, then 75%, on to 50%, and eventually down to a 15% appointment. I am still a research associate professor in the Department of Family Medicine, School of Medicine, so I have that association with a large, well-regarded university. I'm obligated to work 8 hours a week and draw 15% of what had been my full-time salary. Now, I spend the rest of my work hours directing conferences and consulting on a wide variety of campuses. When asked where I work, I still say "UNC," even though it is only 15% of my overall work. In academe, we rarely talk about doing consulting and alt-ac positions as a primary job. The general tone—and I hear it from a lot of people—is if you do not have the university affiliation, you become an independent contractor because you can't get a job or because you have retired. Individuals who do consulting work benefit academe just as faculty members or faculty developers do. The prestige for doing good work as an independent consultant needs to increase. Anything that changes that will be great. (T. Zakrajsek, personal communication, January 15, 2018)

The opportunity to work on conferences and individual consulting, like we talked about in chapter 20, is one that requires a great deal of planning. Look back at your goals for your alt-ac work. Whether you want to write, speak, or consult—full- or part-time—write down tasks that you would like to reduce in your work life to make time for those pursuits. Then, identify one of the areas you listed as the most likely to be manageable. Commit to a conversation with a trusted colleague or group about how to make the change.

Successful Alt-Acs Prefer Opportunities Where They Are Valued

The alt-ac career spectrum ranges from full-time single-employer jobs all the way to independent consulting and part-time alt-ac work. The common thread among all of the alt-ac practitioners whom the authors know is our focus on the concept of value. The majority of alt-ac people are in serving professions, and this eighth and final opportunity has to do with how we define *value*—gravitating toward roles where our skills are valued, as well as work where we can create value for others. When Zakrajsek rebalanced his career, he found that going even further into the alt-ac space was a way to both give back to the profession and find value for himself.

> The concept of stepping away from academe was really frightening to me. It wasn't just difficult (it was very difficult), but it was also totally foreign. I keep thinking that when I'm done playing in this consulting world, I'm going to go back and find a full-time job and become a faculty developer again, because that's what you do. Little by little, what I am realizing is that I will have so much more of an impact on higher education this year, though, by speaking and consulting than I would ever have been able to do as the executive director of the Center for Faculty Excellence. What I am now doing is much more in alignment with my natural strengths.
>
> Unless faculty members donate their salaries back to the university or work for free, they're being paid to do something. And we alt-ac people are also being paid to do something. The difference is that a single university doesn't give us our money: A whole bunch of universities each gives us a little bit. My salary last year was just divvied up amongst 40 different schools. And when we frame it like that, I think we are essentially the same as any full-time faculty member at a university. (T. Zakrajsek, personal communication, January 15, 2018)

The lesson to take away here is to select and respond to opportunities with both personal and other-focused values in mind. Write down two tasks or projects in your desired alt-ac field that you are working on or would like to explore. Then reflect on the value that such work provides to your personal career (e.g., in terms of prestige, recognition, or standing among your peers) and to others in your alt-ac field (e.g., think about collaborations, the ability to reach a wide audience, and how to simplify complex topics and invite others to experiment with them). Think about the balance between personal and outward value when planning your alt-ac career moves.

A Charge to Set You on Your Alt-Ac Path

Although you are finishing this book, you are really just getting started. If you have read through the chapters without taking notes and planning concrete steps, we strongly encourage you to start actually mapping your trajectory within the alt-ac career space. As many of the alt-ac professionals in our profiles have shared, there are many exciting opportunities through which you can achieve your professional and personal goals in academically oriented environments—all without a tenure-track position. Moreover, you are not alone. Rely on peers, mentors, and professional communities for advice and support (and be that kind of support for them, too). Our charge to you is to use the many activities and resources shared in this book to keep moving forward, up, and on.

Contact information for all three authors is included in the "About the Authors" section at the end of this book. We would love to hear from you about your situation and your next steps, and we wish you success and satisfaction with whatever comes next for you in your alt-ac work!

REFERENCES

American Association of University Professors. (2016). Background facts on contingent faculty positions. Retrieved from https://www.aaup.org/issues/contingency/background-facts

Baker, K. J. (2014a, July 15). On "poor husbands" and two-body problems [Blog post]. *Chronicle Vitae*. Retrieved from https://chroniclevitae.com/news/609-on-poor-husbands-and-two-body-problems

Baker, K. J. (2014b, July 15). The two-body problem and us [Blog post]. *Chronicle Vitae*. Retrieved from https://chroniclevitae.com/news/608-the-two-body-problem-and-us

Ball, D. M., Gleason, W., & Peterson, N. J. (2015). From all sides: Rethinking professionalization in a changing job market. *Pedagogy, 15*(1), 103–118.

Belcher, W. (2009). *Writing your journal article in 12 weeks.* Thousand Oaks, CA: Sage.

Bethman, B., & Longstreet, C. S. (2013, May 22). Defining terms: The alt-ac track. *Inside Higher Ed*. Retrieved from https://www.insidehighered.com/advice/2013/05/22/essay-defining-alt-ac-new-phd-job-searches

Bhattarai, A. (2017, July 3). Side hustles are the new norm. *Washington Post*. Retrieved from https://www.washingtonpost.com/news/business/wp/2017/07/03/side-hustles-are-the-new-norm-heres-how-much-they-really-pay/

Bodenheimer, R. M. (2017, August 29). The plight of the independent scholar [Blog post]. *Inside Higher Ed*. Retrieved from https://www.insidehighered.com/advice/2017/08/29/difficulties-and-frustrations-attending-academic-conference-independent-scholar

Bolles, R. N. (2018). *What color is your parachute? 2018: A practical manual for job-hunters and career-changers.* New York, NY: Random House.

Bond, A. (2013, June 10). The (not-so-fabulous) life of gay academics [Blog post]. Retrieved from https://labandfield.wordpress.com/2013/06/10/the-not-so-fabulous-life-of-gay-academics/

Boogaard, K. (n.d.). How I convinced my loved ones that my crazy career change wasn't all that crazy. *The Muse*. Retrieved from https://www.themuse.com/advice/how-i-convinced-my-loved-ones-that-my-crazy-career-change-wasnt-all-that-crazy

Boss, J. (2015, September 11). Find your niche in 60 minutes or less with these 4 questions. *Entrepreneur*. Retrieved from https://www.entrepreneur.com/article/250494

Brown, B. (2012). *Daring greatly: How the courage to be vulnerable transforms the way we live, love, parent and lead.* New York, NY: Avery.

Brown, D. (2016). Professionalizing the first steps of the teaching journey. *Phi Delta Kappan, 98*(1), 31–35.

Butin, D. (2016, January 13). So you want to be a dean? *The Chronicle of Higher Education.* Retrieved from https://www.chronicle.com/article/So-You-Want-to-Be-a-Dean-/234900

Caldwell, B. D. (2014, February). Moving into administration: Should you stay or should you go? [Blog post]. *ASBMB Today.* Retrieved from http://www.asbmb .org/asbmbtoday/201402/ProfessionalDevelopment/

Carter, J. (2013). *The message of you: Turn your life story into a money-making speaking career.* New York, NY: St. Martin's Press.

Carter, J. L. (2016). CCCC chair's address: Making, disrupting, innovating. *College Composition and Communication, 68*(2), 378–408. Retrieved from https:// www.ncte.org/library/NCTEFiles/Resources/Journals/CCC/0682-dec2016/ CCC0682Address.pdf

Chiuri, W. (2012, June 6). 7 steps to find your niche—and dare to risk [Guest blog post]. *Forbes.* Retrieved from https://www.forbes.com/sites/women2/2012/06/ 06/590/#5699adf57816

Chohan, U. W. (2016, January 14). Young, educated and underemployed: Are we building a nation of PhD baristas? *The Conversation.* Retrieved from http:// theconversation.com/young-educated-and-underemployed-are-we-building-a-nation-of-phd-baristas-53104

Clark, D. (2015). *Stand out: How to find your breakthrough idea and build a following around it.* New York, NY: Portfolio/Penguin.

Clark, D. (2017). *Entrepreneurial you.* Boston, MA: HBR Press.

Coetzee, M., & Harry, N. (2014). Emotional intelligence as a predictor of employees' career adaptability. *Journal of Vocational Behavior, 84*(1), 90–97.

Committee on Appointment and Promotions. (2017, October). *Internal guidelines for faculty appointments and promotions.* Columbia University. Retrieved from https://www.mailman.columbia.edu/sites/default/files/pdf/03_coap_guidelines .pdf

Committee on Promotion Tracks. (2015). *Guidebook: Criteria for faculty appointment and promotion.* Cornell University. Retrieved from http://weill.cornell.edu/ ofa/docs/Guidebook_April_2015.pdf

Conway, K. (2005). Mentoring: Back to the basics. *Training, 42*(8), 42.

Cousins, L. P. (2011). Recovering from the loss of a dream [Blog post]. *Psych Central.* Retrieved from https://blogs.psychcentral.com/always-learning/2011/ 01/recovering-from-the-loss-of-a-dream/

Croxall, B. (2013, September 24). What's your speaking fee? [Blog post]. *The Chronicle of Higher Education.* Retrieved from http://www.chronicle.com/blogs/ profhacker/whats-your-speaking-fee/52531

Csikszentmihalyi, M. (2009). *Flow: The psychology of optimal experience.* New York, NY: HarperCollins.

Dillinger, T., Maxfield, A., & Peterson, S. (2017, October 23). A new way for PhDs to plan their careers. *Inside Higher Ed.* Retrieved from https://www.insidehighered.com/advice/2017/10/23/introduction-new-career- exploration-and-planning-tool-phds-essay

DiPietro, M. (2015). Spirit of POD Award. *40th Annual POD Conference.* Award acceptance speech given at 2015 Professional and Organizational Development (POD) Network conference, San Francisco, CA.

Doran, J., & Brizee, A. (2012, May 8). Writing the personal statement. *Purdue Online Writing Lab.* Retrieved from https://owl.purdue.edu/owl/job_search_writing/preparing_an_application/writing_the_personal_statement/index.html

Edmonds, D. (2015, May 28). More than half of college faculty are adjuncts: Should you care? *Forbes.* Retrieved from https://www.forbes.com/sites/noodleeducation/2015/05/28/more-than-half-of-college-faculty-are-adjuncts-should-you-care/#fd0cc3816005

Faculty Affairs Office. (2018). *Information guide for appointments, promotion, and tenure (APT).* Northwestern University. Retrieved from http://www.feinberg.northwestern.edu/fao/docs/admin-general/Information-Guide-for-APT.pdf

Faculty Senate. (2008). *Requirements for appointment, reappointment, promotion, and tenure for full-time tenure-track faculty.* University of Colorado at Denver. Retrieved from http://www.ucdenver.edu/academics/colleges/dentalmedicine/Documents/AppointmentReappointmentPromotionTenure.pdf

Fertik, M., & Thompson, D. C. (2015). *The reputation economy: How to optimize your digital footprint in a world where your reputation is your most valuable asset.* New York, NY: Crown.

Flint, K., & Phillips, C. J. (2018). *Developing a postdoctoral mentoring plan.* National Postdoctoral Association. Retrieved from http://www.nationalpostdoc.org/?MentoringPlans

Fox, B. J. (2015, December 7). How can you overcome the death of a dream? A four step guide [Blog post]. Retrieved from http://www.brettjfox.com/how-can-you-overcome-the-death-of-a-dream-a-four-step-guide/

Gamboa, C. (2012, June 19). How to turn your dissertation, thesis or paper into a publication (part four) [Blog post]. Retrieved from https://connection.sagepub.com/blog/sage-connection/2012/06/19/how-to- turn-your-dissertation-thesis-or-paper-into-a-publication-part-four/

Gastel, B. (2013). Preparing the literature review section of a dissertation [PowerPoint slides]. Retrieved from http://www.authoraid.info/uploads/resources/preparing-the-literature-review-section-of-a-dissertation.pdf

Germano, W. (2013). *From dissertation to book.* Chicago, IL: University of Chicago Press.

Giller, G. (2014, March 26). Couples finding work in the same city: It ain't easy [Poll results]. *Scientific American.* Retrieved from https://blogs.scientificamerican.com/observations/couples-finding-work-in-the-same-city-it-aint-easy-poll-results/

Gillespie, P. (2017, May 24). Intuit: Gig economy is 34% of U.S. workforce. *CNN Money.* Retrieved from http://money.cnn.com/2017/05/24/news/economy/gig-economy-intuit/

Ginder, S. A., Kelly-Reid, J. E., & Mann, F. B. (2018, November). *Enrollment and employees in postsecondary institutions, fall 2017; and financial statistics and academic libraries, fiscal year 2017* (NCES Publication No. NCES 2019-021). Washington, DC: U.S. Department of Education.

Goldsmith, J. A., Komlos, J., & Schine Gold, P. (2010). *The Chicago guide to your academic career: A portable mentor for scholars from graduate school through tenure.* Chicago, IL: University of Chicago Press.

Goldsmith, M., & Reiter, M. (2007). *What got you here won't get you there: How successful people become even more successful.* New York, NY: Hachette Books.

Graduate Career Consortium. (2018). *ImaginePhD.* Retrieved from https://www .imaginephd.com/

Grafton, A. T., & Grossman, J. (2011). No more plan B: A very modest proposal for graduate programs in history. *Perspectives on History: The Newsmagazine of the American Historical Association.* Retrieved from https://www.historians .org/publications-and-directories/perspectives-on-history/october-2011/ no-more-plan-b

Granovetter, M. (1973). The strength of weak ties. *American Journal of Sociology, 78*(6), 1360–1380.

Gray, P., & Drew, D. E. (2012). *What they didn't teach you in graduate school: 299 helpful hints for success in your academic career.* Sterling, VA: Stylus.

Griffey, T. (2017, January 9). The decline of faculty tenure: Less from an oversupply of PhDs, and more from the systematic de-valuation of the PhD as a credential for college teaching. *LaborOnline.* The Labor and Working-Class History Association. Retrieved from https://www.lawcha.org/2017/01/09/ decline-faculty-tenure-less-oversupply-phds-systematic-de-valuation-phd- credential-college-teaching/

Harrington, R. (2015, March 20). Confronting the 2-body problem [Poll results]. *Scientific American.* Retrieved from https://www.scientificamerican.com/article/ confronting-the-2-body-career-problem-poll-results/

Harvard Department of Psychology. (n.d.). Three-paper option. Retrieved from https://psychology.fas.harvard.edu/three-paper-option

Haviland, D., Ortiz, A. M., & Henriques, L. (2017). *Shaping your career: A guide for early career faculty.* Sterling, VA: Stylus.

Hayzlett, J. (2012, January 2). Why you need a better elevator pitch. *Harvard Business Review.* Retrieved from https://hbr.org/2012/01/why-you-need-a-better-elevator/

Hermann, R. (2016, November 16). Impostor syndrome is definitely a thing. *The Chronicle of Higher Education.* Retrieved from https://www.chronicle.com/article/ Impostor-Syndrome-Is/238418

Heyl, J. D., & Damron, D. (2014). Should I stay or should I go? *International Educator, 23*(5), 50–53.

HigherEdJobs. (2013, August). *Higher education employment report: Second quarter, 2013.* Retrieved from https://www.higheredjobs.com/documents/HEJ_ Employment_Report_2013_Q2.pdf

Hoffman, R., & Casnocha, B. (2012, January 24). The real way to build a social network. *Fortune.* Retrieved from http://fortune.com/2012/01/24/the-real-way-to-build-a-social-network/

Hogshead, S. (2014). *How the world sees you: Discover your highest value through the science of fascination.* New York, NY: HarperBusiness.

Hogshead, S. (2016). *Fascinate: How to make your brand impossible to resist.* New York, NY: HarperBusiness.

Iraj, H. (n.d.). How to turn your MA or PhD thesis into a popular book [Blog post]. *The Scholarpreneur.* Retrieved from http://thescholarpreneur.com/guest-post-how-to-turn-your-ma-or-phd-thesis-into-a-popular-book/

Jaschik, S. (2018, January 5). The PhD skill mismatch. *Inside Higher Ed.* Retrieved from https://www.insidehighered.com/news/2018/01/05/study-shows-academic-job-searches-languages-value-alt-ac-skills

Jiménez, J., & Escalante, J. (2017). A non-linear model for career development in academia. *Journal of Unschooling and Alternative Learning, 10*(21), 29–50.

Katzen, M. (1974). *The moosewood cookbook.* New York, NY: Ten Speed press.

Kelsky, K. (2011, July 21). Here's what goes into your tenure portfolio—a special request post [Blog post]. *The Professor Is In.* Retrieved from https://www.theprofessorisin.com/2011/07/21/your-tenure-dossier/

Kim, J. (2016, September 15). The 5 stages of an alt-ac career [Blog post]. *Inside Higher Ed.* Retrieved from https://www.insidehighered.com/blogs/technology-and-learning/5-stages-alt-ac-career

Kim, J. (2017, October 4). If it isn't counted, does it count? *Inside Higher Ed.* Retrieved from https://www.insidehighered.com/digital-learning/blogs/work-alternative-academics-mostly-invisible

Kübler-Ross, E. (1969). *On death and dying.* New York, NY: Scribner.

Kuhn, C., & Castaño, Z. (2016). Boosting the career development of postdocs with a peer-to-peer mentor circles program. *Nature Biotechnology, 34*(7), 781–783.

Laurence, D. (2016, November 17). Employment trends in higher education workforce: IPEDS data on growth in administrators, other nonteaching professionals, and the faculty [Blog post]. MLA Office of Research. Retrieved from https://mlaresearch.mla.hcommons.org/2016/11/17/employment-trends-in-the-higher-education-workforce-ipeds-data-on-growth-in-administrators-other-nonteaching-professionals-and-the-faculty/

Lazuli. (2014, September 19). Don't follow in my footsteps: A reverse roadmap for women in academia and beyond [Blog post]. Retrieved from https://andwhatt odowiththebooks.wordpress.com/2014/09/19/dont-follow-in-my-footsteps-a-reverse-roadmap-for-women-in-academia-and-beyond/

Linder, K. E. (2018). *Managing your professional identity online: A guide for higher education.* Sterling, VA: Stylus.

LinkedIn Corporate Communications Team. (2017, June 22). Eighty percent of professionals consider networking important to career success [Web article]. Retrieved from https://news.linkedin.com/2017/6/eighty-percent-of-professionals-consider-networking-important-to-career-success

Lobosco, K. (2017, June 29). Illinois is starving state colleges and universities. *CNN Money.* Retrieved from http://money.cnn.com/2017/06/29/pf/college/illinois-budget-higher-education/

Ma-Kellams, C., & Lerner, J. (2016). Trust your gut or think carefully? Examining whether an intuitive versus a systematic mode of thought produces greater empathic accuracy. *Journal of Personality and Social Psychology, 111*(5), 674–685.

Malhotra, D. (2012). *Tragedy and genius.* Harvard business school. Retrieved from https://youtu.be/D73mm29XXAw

Martin, J. W., & Hughes, B. (2012). Small *p* publishing: A networked blogging approach to academic discourse. *Journal of Electronic Resources Librarianship, 24*(1), 17–21.

Maslow, A. H. (1943). A theory of human motivation. *Psychological Review, 50*(4), 370–396. Retrieved from http://psychclassics.yorku.ca/Maslow/motivation.htm

McGinn, E. (2016, June 21). Comparative literature, digital humanities, and the interstitial PhD [Blog post]. Connected Academics. Retrieved from https://connect.mla.hcommons.org/interstitialphd/

McNeil, L., & Sher, M. (2001, January). The two-body problem, part II: Seeking employment solutions for dual-science-career couples [Web article]. American Astronomical Society. Retrieved from https://cswa.aas.org/status/2001/JANUARY2001/McNeilandSher.html

Miller, J. (n.d.). Know your niche: 5 leadership quotes about finding your career sweet spot [Web article]. *Be Leaderly.* Retrieved from http://www.beleaderly.com/know-your-niche-5-leadership-quotes-about-finding-your-career-sweet-spot/

Miller, M. D. (2018, February 22). Forget mentors—What we really need are fans [Blog post]. *The Chronicle of Higher Education.* Retrieved from https://www.chronicle.com/article/Forget-Mentors-What-We/242597

National Center for Education Statistics. (2018). *Integrated postsecondary education data system.* Washington, DC: U.S. Department of Education. Retrieved from https://nces.ed.gov/ipeds

Newport, C. (2012). *So good they can't ignore you: Why skills trump passion in the quest for work you love.* New York, NY: Hachette Book Group.

Nungsari, M. (2017, June 18). We solved our 2-body problem—by moving to Malaysia [Web article]. *The Chronicle of Higher Education.* Retrieved from https://www.chronicle.com/article/We-Solved-Our-2-Body-Problem/240389

Office of the Provost. (2018). Appointment and promotion. University of Chicago. Retrieved from https://provost.uchicago.edu/handbook/academic-appointments/appointment-and-promotion#546

Parrinello-Cason, M. (2012, August 23). Women, academia and the balancing act [Blog post]. Retrieved from http://www.balancingjane.com/2012/08/women-academia-and-balancing-act.html

Patsopoulos, N. A., Analatos, A. A., & Ioannidis, J. P. (2005). Relative citation impact of various study designs in the health sciences. *Journal of the American Medical Association, 293*(19), 2362–2366. Retrieved from https://www.ncbi.nlm.nih.gov/pubmed/15900006

Perlmutter, D. D. (2015, August 12). The completion agenda, part 4: Finishing and the job hunt. *The Chronicle of Higher Education*. Retrieved from https://www.chronicle.com/article/The-Completion-Agenda-Part-4-/232281

Phillips, C. J. (2009, June). *Mentoring plans for postdoctoral associates.* Presented at the National Postdoctoral Association Joint Annual Meeting. Retrieved from http://c.ymcdn.com/sites/www.nationalpostdoc.org/resource/resmgr/Docs/nsf-jam-09.pdf

Pink, D. (2012). *To sell is human.* New York, NY: Riverhead Books.

Polka, L. (2003, April). Psychologists in non-traditional academic departments. *American Psychological Observer*. Retrieved from https://www.psychologicalscience.org/observer/psychologists-in-non-traditional-academic-departments-2

Reed, M. (2013, October 3). Two bodies, one job [Web article]. *Slate*. Retrieved from http://www.slate.com/articles/life/inside_higher_ed/2013/10/academia_s_confounding_two_body_problem.html

Reed, M. (2018, January 31). The two-body problem revisited [Blog post]. *Inside Higher Ed*. Retrieved from https://www.insidehighered.com/blogs/confessions-community-college-dean/two-body-problem-revisited

Rhodes, C., & Butler, J. S. (2010). Organizational membership and business success: The importance of networking and moving beyond homophily. *Challenge, 16*(1), 33–48.

Rivera, L. A. (2017). When two bodies are (not) a problem: Gender and relationship status discrimination in academic hiring. *American Sociological Review, 82*(6), 1111–1138.

Robinson, D. L. (2008). Brain function, emotional experience and personality. *Netherlands Journal of Psychology, 64*(4), 152–168.

Rockquemore, K. A. (2017, October 25). Posttenure mentoring networks. *Inside Higher Ed*. Retrieved from https://www.insidehighered.com/advice/2017/10/25/building-network-mentors-after-you-receive-tenure-essay

Rogers, K. (n.d.). Who we are. Retrieved from http://altacademy.wufoo.com/forms/who-we-are/

Sandberg, S. (2017). *Option B: Facing adversity, building resilience, and finding joy.* New York, NY: Knopf.

Schiebinger, L., Henderson, A. D., & Gilmartin, S. K. (2008). *Dual career academic couples: What universities need to know.* Palo Alto, CA: Michelle R. Clayman Institute for Gender Research, Stanford University. Retrieved from https://gender.stanford.edu/sites/g/files/sbiybj5961/f/publications/dualcareer-final_0.pdf

Seltzer, B. (2016, March 1). The strength of the alt-ac candidate on the academic market [Blog post]. *Connected Academics*. Retrieved from https://connect.mla.hcommons.org/the-strength-of-the-altac-candidate-on-the-academic-market/

Shankman, P. (2015). *Zombie loyalists: Using great service to create rabid fans.* New York, NY: Palgrave Macmillan.

Shehata, A., Ellis, D., & Foster, A. E. (2017). Changing styles of informal academic communication in the age of the web. *Journal of Documentation, 73*(5), 825–842.

Simon, C. (2016). *Impossible to ignore: Creating memorable content to influence decisions.* New York, NY: McGraw Hill Education.

Snow, S. (2014, October 7). What we learned from sending 1,000 cold e-mails. *Fast Company.* Retrieved from https://www.fastcompany.com/3036672/what-we-learned-from-sending-1000-cold-e-mails

Sorcinelli, M. D., & Yun, J. (2007). From mentor to mentoring networks: Mentoring in the new academy. *Change: The Magazine of Higher Learning, 39*(6), 58–61.

Stanley, N. (n.d.). How to tell your friends and family about your career change. *Careershifters.* Retrieved from https://www.careershifters.org/expert-advice/how-to-tell-your-friends-and-family-about-your-career-change

Stone, D., Patton, B., & Heen, S. (2010). *Difficult conversations: How to discuss what matters most.* New York, NY: Penguin.

Strouse, A. W. (2017, March 8). Transcending the job market. *The Chronicle of Higher Education.* Retrieved from http://www.chronicle.com/article/Transcending-the-Job-Market/239407

Sur, A. (n.d.). Top 10 list of alternative careers for PhD science graduates [Blog post]. *Cheeky Scientist.* Retrieved from https://cheekyscientist.com/top-10-list-of-alternative-careers-for-phd-science-graduates/

The Regents of the University of Michigan. (2018). *How to mentor graduate students: A guide for faculty.* Dearborn, MI: University of Michigan. Retrieved from https://www.rackham.umich.edu/downloads/publications/Fmentoring.pdf

Thomas, B., & Skinner, H. (2012). Dissertation to journal article: A systematic approach. *Education Research International.* Retrieved from https://www.hindawi.com/journals/edri/2012/862135/

Tobin, T. J. (2000, September 22). Technology in the classroom: Time-critical online-course development. *Technology and innovation across the curriculum.* Western Pennsylvania Community College Resource Consortium (WPCCRC) Conference. Youngwood, PA: Westmoreland County Community College. Retrieved from http://mathcs.duq.edu/~tobin/cv/essay.tiac.01.ppt

Tobin, T. J. (2001a). *Technology in the classroom.* Monaca, PA: Community College of Beaver County. Retrieved from http://mathcs.duq.edu/~tobin/cv/essay.ccbc.01.rtf

Tobin, T. J. (2001b). *Technology and community* [Community Discussion series]. Pittsburgh, PA: Pennsylvania Humanities Council. Retrieved from https://web.archive.org/web/20040417221013/http://pahumanities.org/technology.php

Tobin, T. J. (2014). Training your faculty about copyright when the lawyer isn't looking. *Online Journal of Distance Learning Administration, 17(2).* Retrieved from http://www.westga.edu/~distance/ojdla/summer172/tobin172.html

Tobin, T. J. (2018). Speaking brochure. Retrieved from http://mathcs.duq.edu/~tobin/cv/Tobin.Speaking.Brochure.pdf

Tribe, R., & Tunariu, A. (2016). Turning your dissertation into a publishable journal article. *Counseling Psychology Review, 31*(1), 50–58. Retrieved from https://www.researchgate.net/publication/304484755_Turning_your_dissertation_into_a_publishable_journal_article

U.S. Government Accountability Office. (2017, October 19). *Contingent workforce: Size, characteristics, compensation, and work experiences of adjunct and other non-tenure-track faculty* (Report to Congressional Requesters: GAO-18-49). Washington, DC: Author. Retrieved from https://www.gao.gov/products/GAO-18-49.

Vailiancourt, A. M. (2013, October 18). Why did you leave so soon? *The Chronicle of Higher Education, 60*(7), 53.

Van Wyck, J. M. (2018, June 11). How graduate advisers can bolster their career guidance. *Inside Higher Ed.* Retrieved from https://www.insidehighered.com/advice/2018/06/11/ways-advisers-can-better-inform-phd-students-careers-today-opinion

Wapnick, E. (2017). *How to be everything: A guide for those who (still) don't know what they want to be when they grow up.* New York, NY: HarperCollins.

Warner, J. (2017, March 15). My after-academic role models. *Inside Higher Ed.* Retrieved from https://www.insidehighered.com/blogs/just-visiting/my-after-academia-role-models

Whitmer, J. C. (2013). *Logging on to improve achievement: Evaluating the relationship between use of the learning management system, student characteristics, and academic achievement in a hybrid large enrollment undergraduate course* (PhD thesis, University of California, Davis). Retrieved from https://www.learntechlib.org/p/121047/

Williams, L., & Haley, E. (2018, June 18). Grieving the loss of hopes and dreams [Blog post]. *What's Your Grief?* Retrieved from https://whatsyourgrief.com/loss-of-hopes-and-dreams/

Williams, T. (n.d.). Perks of working in higher education [Blog post]. *LiveCareer.* Retrieved from https://www.livecareer.com/quintessential/working-higher-education

Wing, M. R. (2017). *Passion projects for smart people.* Fresno, CA: Quill Driver Books.

Wöhrer, V. (2014). To stay or to go? Narratives of early-stage sociologists about persisting in academia. *Higher Education Policy, 27*(4), 469–487.

Zachary, L. (2009). *The mentee's guide: Making mentoring work for you.* San Francisco, CA: Jossey-Bass.

Zachary, L. (2011). *The mentor's guide: Facilitating effective learning relationships* (2nd ed). San Francisco, CA: Jossey-Bass.

Zhang, H., & Kmec, J. A. (2018). Non-normative connections between work and family: the gendered career consequences of being a dual-career academic. *Sociological Perspectives, 61*(5), 766–786. Retrieved from https://doi.org/10.1177/0731121418778534

Zipkin, A. (2015, February 6). Consulting as a bridge between full-time work and retirement. *New York Times.* Retrieved from https://www.nytimes.com/2015/02/07/your-money/consulting-as-a-bridge-between-full-time-work-and-retirement.html

ABOUT THE AUTHORS

Kathryn E. Linder is the director of the Ecampus Research Unit at Oregon State University. She is a certified life and work coach through the International Coach Federation.

Linder is an avid writer and researcher with a passion for process and peeking behind the scenes at what it takes to be a successful academic. For the past several years, her work has focused on blended course design best practices, institutional supports for accessible online learning, and research literacy for scholarship of teaching and learning practitioners and distance education stakeholders. She speaks on topics related to writing and publication, creativity and productivity, self-promotion and personal branding, and teaching and learning with technology.

Her latest works include the edited collection *The Business of Innovating Online* (Stylus, 2019), *Managing Your Professional Identity Online* (Stylus, 2018), *High-Impact Practices in Online Education* (Stylus, 2018; coedited with Chrysanthemum Mattison Hayes), the edited *New Directions* volume on *Hybrid Teaching and Learning* (Wiley, 2017), and *The Blended Course Design Workbook* (Stylus, 2016). She is also the editor of a forthcoming book series, Thrive Online, due for release from Stylus in 2019. Linder is also the creator of SoTL by Design (https://sotlbydesign.com), a comprehensive online course on designing and implementing scholarship of teaching and learning projects.

Linder earned her BA in English literature from Whitworth University in Spokane, Washington, and her MA and PhD in women's, gender, and sexuality studies from The Ohio State University.

Visit https://drkatielinder.com to learn more about Linder's work and projects.

Kevin Kelly, throughout almost 20 years in higher education, has worked in alt-ac roles—both on and beyond campuses—by advancing and supporting higher education faculty and campus leaders, nationally and internationally. Although he started consulting through side gigs, he now works full-time as a higher education consultant, specializing in both common and niche areas, like teaching and learning (with or without technology), distance education, equity and inclusion, academic technology adoption and implementation, strategic planning, professional and leadership development, and more. He participates in many communities, helping organize conferences, serving as a board member for both professional associations and start-ups, and contributing to online discussions and social media groups.

He continues to teach graduate and undergraduate courses as a part-time lecturer at San Francisco State University, where he has taught since 1999. His current research interests relate to increasing student success and retention, reducing equity and achievement gaps in online courses, and fostering metacognition.

He has been a leader at 2 different organizations established to support faculty and student success at higher education institutions through professional and leadership development. Prior to his full-time positions outside of academia, Kelly served for over 12 years at San Francisco State University, managing 2 Academic Technology teams, leading the faculty development center, and codirecting a U.S. Department of Education grant project.

He has published numerous peer-reviewed book chapters and journal articles related to teaching, learning, and technology and was a lead editor of the collaboratively authored book *Education for a Digital World 2.0: Innovations in Education* (Crown, 2011). He also publishes online courses for the Education channel at LinkedIn Learning/Lynda.com.

Kelly was a Regents Scholar at the University of California, Santa Cruz, where he earned his BA in American studies. He holds an MA in instructional technologies from San Francisco State University and an EdD in organization and leadership from the University of San Francisco.

Thomas J. Tobin is the program area director of distance teaching and learning for the Learning Design, Development, & Innovation (LDDI) team in the Division of Continuing Studies at the University of Wisconsin–Madison (UW-Madison), as well as an internationally recognized speaker and author on topics related to quality in technology-enhanced education, especially copyright, evaluation of teaching practice, academic integrity, and accessibility and universal design for learning.

Before joining UW–Madison, Tobin spent seven years in the learning and development arm of Blue Cross and Blue Shield of Illinois and then served for five years as the coordinator of learning technologies in the Center for Teaching and Learning (CTL) at Northeastern Illinois University in Chicago.

Since the advent of online courses in higher education in the late 1990s, Tobin's work has focused on using technology to extend the reach of higher education beyond its traditional audience. He advocates for the educational rights of people with disabilities and people from disadvantaged backgrounds.

He holds a PhD in English literature, a second MA in information science, a project management professional (PMP) certification, a master online teacher (MOT) certification, and the Quality Matters reviewer certification. He recently earned his Certified Professional in Accessibility Core Competencies (CPACC) credential (he tells his nieces and nephews that he is in the 42nd grade).

Tobin serves on the editorial boards of *InSight: A Journal of Scholarly Teaching*, the *Journal of Interactive Online Learning*, and the *Online Journal of Distance Learning Administration*.

His other books include *Evaluating Online Teaching: Implementing Best Practices* (Wiley, 2015) with Jean Mandernach and Ann H. Taylor; *The Copyright Ninja: Rise of the Ninja* (St. Aubin Comics, 2017); and *Reach Everyone, Teach Everyone: Universal Design for Learning in Higher Education* (West Virginia University Press, 2018) with Kirsten Behling.

Tobin was also proud to represent the United States on a spring 2018 Fulbright Scholar fellowship, under which he helped Eötvös Loránd University in Budapest, Hungary, develop its first faculty development program, and he provided workshops and training to six other universities throughout Hungary, as well as the Hungarian army.

Tobin speaks and consults worldwide. Visit http://thomasjtobin.com for more information on Tobin's projects.

INDEX

Faculty Development books from Stylus Publishing

Advancing the Culture of Teaching on Campus
ow a Teaching Center Can Make a Difference
Edited by Constance Cook and Matthew Kaplan
Foreword by Lester P. Monts

Faculty Mentoring
A Practical Manual for Mentors, Mentees, Administrators, and Faculty Developers
Susan L. Phillips and Susan T. Dennison
Foreword by Milton D. Cox

Faculty Retirement
Best Practices for Navigating the Transition
Edited by Claire Van Ummersen, Jean McLaughlin and Lauren Duranleau
Foreword by Lotte Bailyn

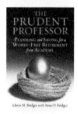

The Prudent Professor
Planning and Saving for a Worry-Free Retirement from Academe
Edwin M. Bridges and Brian D. Bridges

Teaching Across Cultural Strengths
A Guide to Balancing Integrated and Individuated Cultural Frameworks in College Teaching
Alicia Fedelina Chávez and Susan Diana Longerbeam
Foreword by Joseph L. White

Why Students Resist Learning
A Practical Model for Understanding and Helping Students
Edited by Anton O. Tolman and Janine Kremling
Foreword by John Tagg

Graduate and Doctoral Education books from Stylus Publishing

From Diplomas to Doctorates
The Success of Black Women in Higher Education and its Implications for Equal Educational Opportunities for All
Edited by V. Barbara Bush, Crystal Renee Chambers, and Mary Beth Walpole

The Latina/o Pathway to the Ph.D.
Abriendo Caminos
Edited by Jeanett Castellanos, Alberta M. Gloria, and Mark Kamimura
Foreword by Melba Vasquez and Hector Garza

On Becoming a Scholar
Socialization and Development in Doctoral Education
Jay Caulfield
Edited by Susan K. Gardner and Pilar Mendoza
Foreword by Ann E. Austin and Kevin Kruger

Developing Quality Dissertations in the Humanities
A Graduate Student's Guide to Achieving Excellence
Barbara E. Lovitts and Ellen L. Wert

Developing Quality Dissertations in the Sciences
A Graduate Student's Guide to Achieving Excellence
Barbara E. Lovitts and Ellen L. Wert

Developing Quality Dissertations in the Social Sciences
A Graduate Student's Guide to Achieving Excellence
Barbara E. Lovitts and Ellen L. Wert

General Interest books from Stylus Publishing

Are You Smart Enough?
How Colleges' Obsession with Smartness Shortchanges Students
Alexander W. Astin

The New Science of Learning
How to Learn in Harmony With Your Brain
Terry Doyle and Todd D. Zakrajsek
Foreword by Kathleen F. Gabriel

Of Education, Fishbowls, and Rabbit Holes
Rethinking Teaching and Liberal Education for an Interconnected World
Jane Fried with Peter Troiano
Foreword by Dawn R. Person

Managing Your Professional Identity Online
A Guide for Faculty, Staff, and Administrators
Kathryn E. Linder
Foreword by Laura Pasquini

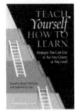

Teach Yourself How to Learn
Strategies You Can Use to Ace Any Course at Any Level
Saundra Yancy McGuire with Stephanie McGuire
Foreword by Mark McDaniel

Pitch Perfect
Communicating with Traditional and Social Media for Scholars, Researchers, and Academic Leaders
William Tyson
Foreword by Robert Zemsky

Job Search/Staff Recruitment & Retention books from Stylus Publishing

The Complete Academic Search Manual
A Systematic Approach to Successful and Inclusive Hiring
Lauren A. Vicker and Harriette J. Royer

Debunking the Myth of Job Fit in Higher Education and Student Affairs
Edited by Brian J. Reece, Vu T. Tran, Elliott N. DeVore and Gabby Porcaro
Foreword by Stephen John Quaye

Establishing the Family-Friendly Campus
Models for Effective Practice
Edited by Jaime Lester and Margaret Sallee

Job Search In Academe
How to Get the Position You Deserve
Dawn M. Formo and Cheryl Reed

The New Talent Acquisition Frontier
Integrating HR and Diversity Strategy in the Private and Public Sectors and Higher Education
Edna Chun and Alvin Evans
Foreword by Andy Brantley and Benjamin D. Reese, Jr.

Search Committees
A Comprehensive Guide to Successful Faculty, Staff, and Administrative Searches
Christopher D. Lee
Foreword by Edna Chun

Professional Development books from Stylus Publishing

Adjunct Faculty Voices
Cultivating Professional Development and Community at the Front Lines of Higher Education
Edited by Roy Fuller, Marie Kendall Brown and Kimberly Smith
Foreword by Adrianna Kezar

Authoring Your Life
Developing an INTERNAL VOICE to Navigate Life's Challenges
Marcia B. Baxter Magolda
Foreword by Sharon Daloz Parks
Illustrated by Matthew Henry Hall

The Coach's Guide for Women Professors
Who Want a Successful Career and a Well-Balanced Life
Rena Seltzer
Foreword by Frances Rosenbluth

Contingent Academic Labor
Evaluating Conditions to Improve Student Outcomes
Daniel B. Davis
Foreword by Adrianna Kezar

Shaping Your Career
A Guide for Early Career Faculty
Don Haviland, Anna M. Ortiz and Laura Henriques
Foreword by Ann E. Austin

What They Didn't Teach You in Graduate School
299 Helpful Hints for Success in Your Academic Career
Paul Gray and David E. Drew
Illustrated by Matthew Henry Hall
Foreword by Laurie Richlin and Steadman Upham